797,885 Books

are available to read at

www.ForgottenBooks.com

Forgotten Books' App
Available for mobile, tablet & eReader

ISBN 978-1-333-57312-6
PIBN 10521447

This book is a reproduction of an important historical work. Forgotten Books uses
state-of-the-art technology to digitally reconstruct the work, preserving the original format
whilst repairing imperfections present in the aged copy. In rare cases, an imperfection in
the original, such as a blemish or missing page, may be replicated in our edition. We do,
however, repair the vast majority of imperfections successfully; any imperfections that
remain are intentionally left to preserve the state of such historical works.

Forgotten Books is a registered trademark of FB &c Ltd.
Copyright © 2015 FB &c Ltd.
FB &c Ltd, Dalton House, 60 Windsor Avenue, London, SW19 2RR.
Company number 08720141. Registered in England and Wales.

For support please visit www.forgottenbooks.com

1 MONTH OF
FREE
READING

at

www.ForgottenBooks.com

By purchasing this book you are eligible for one month membership to ForgottenBooks.com, giving you unlimited access to our entire collection of over 700,000 titles via our web site and mobile apps.

To claim your free month visit:

www.forgottenbooks.com/free521447

* Offer is valid for 45 days from date of purchase. Terms and conditions apply.

English
Français
Deutsche
Italiano
Español
Português

www.forgottenbooks.com

Mythology Photography **Fiction**
Fishing Christianity **Art** Cooking
Essays Buddhism Freemasonry
Medicine **Biology** Music **Ancient
Egypt** Evolution Carpentry Physics
Dance Geology **Mathematics** Fitness
Shakespeare **Folklore** Yoga Marketing
Confidence Immortality Biographies
Poetry **Psychology** Witchcraft
Electronics Chemistry History **Law**
Accounting **Philosophy** Anthropology
Alchemy Drama Quantum Mechanics
Atheism Sexual Health **Ancient History**
Entrepreneurship Languages Sport
Paleontology Needlework Islam
Metaphysics Investment Archaeology
Parenting Statistics Criminology
Motivational

T

BOOK OF BRADFORD

CONTAINING A

Condensed History of the City of Bradford, Points
of interest and Facts about the City, and
other Information of Various Kinds.

ALSO A

Complete and Accurate Business Directory.

Railroad Time Tables, Distance and Fare Tables on all Railroads Entering the City, a List of the City Officials, etc,

ISSUED DECEMBER, 1897.

COMPILED AND PUBLISHED BY F. M. MCDONNELL,
BRADFORD, PA.

COPYRIGHTED BY

F. M. McDONNELL.

1897.

WORLD PUB. CO., TITUSVILLE, PA.

PREFACE.

This little work was compiled with the object in view of giving the general public a book of reference pertaining to the various business interests of the city of Bradford, combined with useful information of all kinds, and in a form which would be most convenient. As the work of compiling progressed various ideas were suggested which have been carried out, with the result that the amount of information herein contained is far reater than at first contemplated. The "Historical tes" will be found a most handy and interesting portion of the work, touching, as they do, most of the important events in the history of the city, and being a review of the happenings which have transpired from the time the Tuna Valley was a wilderness to the present ousy days. The railroad information, too, will be at least interesting, if not of practical value, to every one. For the Businnss Directory it can only be said that great care has been taken in the canvass of all the business interests now being conducted in the city, not to overlook a single one, and if such an oversight has occurred it has been unintentional.

THE PUBLISHER.

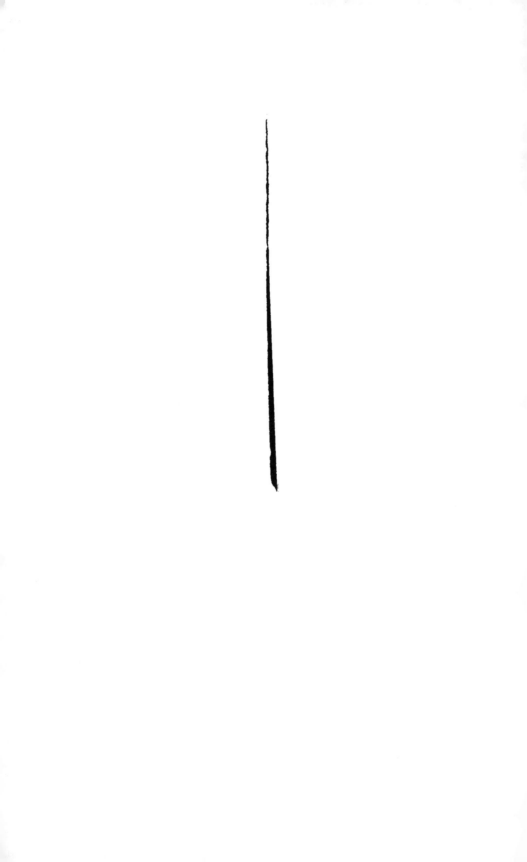

HISTORICAL.

BRADFORD, McKEAN COUNTY.

McKean county is bounded on the north by the New York-Pennsylvania line ; on the east by Potter county ; on the south by Elk and Cameron counties ; on the west by Warren county. The city of Bradford is situated within a few miles of the northern line of McKean county. and about midway between Warren and Potter counties. It stands at the confluence of the East and West Branches of the Tuna, a tributary of the Allegheny river. In 1837 Col. Little purchased 250.000 acres in and around Bradford. and built a log house. In 1838 the village was surveyed and named Littleton. In 1851 Daniel Kingsbury purchased a large tract of land from the United States Land company. and became most active and untiring in his determination to develop the resources of the village. and found a city. In 1858 he had the name Littleton changed to Bradford. and with J. K. Haffey and others established the Bradford Miner. to assist in building up the new city. In 1873 the people asked for borough government and the demand was granted. From this time forward the valley was a scene of the wildest activity. Busy men from all parts of the world crowded into the town in search of fortunes, in the form of petroleum. Thousands of derricks grew up. and all kinds of buildings sprung up like reeds. In 1880 there were eight large brick buildings erected. among them the Riddell House. Over five hundred new dwellings were built and a number of new streets laid out. Since that time the wonderful growth of the city has ceased to become a matter of local history. To-day Bradford is a city of which its citizens are proud.

ANTI-BELLUM DAYS.

Little has ever been written of a historical nature of those early days on the Tunungwant. and before the beginning of the oil excitement. It is generally supposed that Bradford, before the discovery of oil. was an unknown wilderness. As far as being a wilderness. it might be called that, but it was not unknown. A brief sketch of those days is here given. which was kindly furnished by ex-Mayor Loyal Ward. who speaks of them as anti-bellum days. Mr. Ward came to Kendall from the Springville. (N. Y.) Academy in the winter of 1849-50. to teach the Kendall Creek School. Kendall was at that time the great lumber centre of the Tuna valley. The people were most enterprising and intelligent. Methodist. Baptist and Congregational churches were established. The schools Mr. Ward found to be of a higher order than those of his native state. In fact he says that plenty of cheek, a silk hat and strait bodied coat was what carried him through. A vast amount of wealth was centured in the valley. Wealthy, educated men were engaged in the lumber business. John F. Melvin an educated and highly cultured gentleman, (the father of C. C. and F. J. Melvin) was associated with Judge Chamberlain in the lumber and mercantile business. S W. Bradley with Mr. Fay, of Cincinnati, were very prominent men, and large dealers and manufacturers of lumber. Fuller & Miller, Leach & Johnston. William Fisher, Nathan DeGolier, Mr. Webb, Mr. Moore, Frank Irvine, Mr. Fuller, John Whipple, H. W. Barr, Holmes & Porter, Mr. Sutton and others were all engaged in the lumber business. In fact the woods was full of lumber men. Daniel Kingsbury was the central figure. He was the successor to the United States Land Company, and was also extensively engaged in the lumber business and afterwards was instrumental in establishing the McKean County Bank, on the corner of Main and Congress streets. Col. Little, who came to the valley as the agent of the United States Land Company, was also a very prominent citizen. The people lived high, money was plenty and poverty was unknown. The lumber. shingles, lath and square timber were rafted and floated out on the Tunungwant creek and on down the Allegany river to Pittsburg, Cincinnati, Louisville and points further south. One of the grandest sights in nature, Mr. Ward says, were these hills, overtopped with massive Weymoth pines shutting out all other growth, and almost constantly rocking and swaying. Game was plenty. Not an uncommon sight was that of deer feeding in the back fields. In the spring of the year, at high water time, it took an army of men to get the lumber out to the Allegany river. Raftsmen came from all parts to work. And these raftsmen were not without their sport. One night a number of them gathered at Rice's Hotel, and could not get beds to sleep in. So to pass the night pleasantly they made the landlord a prisoner and took a barrel of whisky out and set it on the counter appointing one of their number to act as bartender. The whole barrel was finished before daylight, and the reader can see their finish. Another time C. C. Melvin and a few other sinners were taken to the edge of a raft, somewhat against their will, and baptised by immersion in the water of the creek. As to whether any one of them have ever become backsliders Judge Ward cannot say.

HISTORICAL NOTES.

McKean county was organized in 1804.

The Burt House fire occurred June 19, 1884.

The Masonic Temple was erected in 1889-90.

The Palace Hotel fire occurred January 11, 1889.

Thomas Murphy was first chief of police in 1879.

The First National Bank begun business in 1880.

The first pioneers appeared in the valley in 1823.

The first borough government was established in 1873.

The first observation of Decoration Day was in 1876.

6

Bradford's City Charter was granted January 14, 1879.

The first white child was born in the Tuna Valley in 1828.

The Hart family settled on the site of Bradford about 1827.

The Bradford House was destroyed by fire on May 30, 1868.

The McKean County Bank was chartered May 13, 1857.

The Commercial National Bank was opened in March, 1890.

Electric lights were first turned on in the city January 14, 1890.

The Bradford National Bank commenced business July 25, 1879.

The Young Men's Christian Association was organized May 27, 1889.

The first mayor of the city of Bradford was Hon. James Broder, 1879.

The Bradford Military Company completed enrollment on August 30, 1880.

The Protestant Episcopal church was destroyed by fire on January 19, 1890.

The fatal acccident on the old Peg-leg railroad occurred on January 27, 1879.

The new Erie depot was completed and opened for business on April 6, 1891.

The first church was erected in 1850. and was used by all religious denominations.

The first burgess of Bradford borough was Hon. P. T. Kennedy, in 1873. Deceased.

The town of Littleton, afterwards changed to Bradford, was first surveyed in 1838.

The winter of 1879 was a hummer. Snow fell for seventy-eight consecutive days.

The central office of the United Pipe line was destroyed by fire June 22, 1882. Loss $20,000.

The first grist mill in the Tuna Valley was constructed in 1832 by Nathan DeGolier.

The first building erected in the valley was a log cabin, which was built by William Bennett.

Kendall was named in honor of Amos Kendall, who was Postmaster General at that time.

St. Bernard's new brick church was dedicated by Bishop Mullen, of Erie, Pa., October 8, 1893.

The fire which destroyed Bovaird & Seyfang's boiler shop occurred August 26, 1880. Loss $50,000.

The Bradford Driving Park and Fair Association was permanently organized October 11, 1889.

The Bradford Glass Co.'s plant, on Hilton street, was destroyed by fire Sept. 18, 1896. Loss $12,000.

Friday evening, January 8, 1892, the B. B. & K. R'y shops and several engines were destroyed by fire.

The first newspaper published in Bradford was the "Bradford Miner." by Sam C. Crane: March 12, 1858.

Corporal Thomas Albert, of Co. C, was shot through the heart at the company's range on January 8, 1895.

The Bradford Water Works Company was incorporated in 1877, and in 1879 the plant was sold to the city.

The fire which destroyed the old City Building occurred on the morning of June 15, 1894. No insurance.

The Bradford Oil Exchange (Exchange Lyceum) was erected in 1878-79, at a cost of $44,000 including the lot.

Kendall, or Tarport, was annexed to Bradford and became the Sixth ward of the city, Friday, March 11, 1892.

The Tuna valley was the hunting grounds of the Cornplanter Indians before the advent of the civilized race.

Tarport, now East Bradford, derived its name from a tar and feather party which occurred in its early history.

Sunday evening, January 31, 1892, Jas. W. McCafferty and wife were instantly killed in a railroad accident at Watsonville.

About the year 1878 walking matches were the rage in Bradford. Six-day-go-as-you-please events were quite numerous.

The first store building was erected in the city by Johnson & Melvin, on the southwest corner of Main and Congress streets.

The first oil well drilled in the Bradford field was in 1861, and was located on the north side of Corydon street, near the creek.

The Laurel Steam Fire Company, of York, Pa., visited the city October 23-24, 1894, and were the guests of the F. S. Johnston Hose Co.

The Producers Petroleum Exchange was chartered in December, 1882, and erected in 1883. It was opened for business January 2, 1884.

Abner Arnold was burned to death in the fire of November 27, 1892, when M. W. Wagner's barn, on Congress street, was destroyed.

The public square fire of December, 1882, dstroyed Habernig's store, the Hotel La Pierre; the Hotel Florence, and Irvins' livery stable.

Coal oil, benzole, camphene oil, and tallow was manufactured from coal, in 1859 in buildings opposite the present site of the Riddell House.

The largest fire in the history of the city occurred on Nov. 15-16, 1878, destroying over 40 buildings, including the old Riddel House. Loss $156,000.

The fire of January 9, 1888, started in Bateman's

8

Hotel and burned to Greenewald's Clothing Store and up to the Oil City House. Loss $40,000.

The fire of Reilbey's Hotel and bakery, in which Mrs. Reibley, her two children and a Swedish girl were burned to death, occurred July 11, 1884.

The first annual convention of the Northwestern Pennsylvania Volunteer Firemen's Association was held in Bradford, August 22 and 23, 1895.

Mr. and Mrs. Edward B. Pemberton, Mrs. W. S. Hart and Miss Margaret Henry, all of .Bradford, were drowned at Alexandria Bay July 17, 1890.

Indians continued to visit the village of Littleton up to 1850, coming in large numbers and remaining for days at a time, trading with the villagers.

The glycerine explosion which destroyed the McIntyre Torpedo Company's magazine and killed M. B. Pulver, A. P. Higgins, C. Page and J. B. Burkholder, occurred Sept. 15, 1878, near Toad Hollow.

The fire of April 21, 1891, which destroyed six dwellings on Pleasant street, was the cause of the organization of the Geo. H. Potter Hose Company.

Since the establishment of McKean county, in 1804, three men have been executed. They were Uzza Robbins, Andrew Tracey and Ralph Crossmire.

The Bay State Hotel fire which took in the buildings from McCort's Restaurant to Chestnut street occurred on the night of June 19, 1896. Loss $50,000.

The Higgins House and B. R. & P. depot fire occurred on April 1, 1893. Three persons were burned to death and six seriously, but not fatally. Loss $26,000.

The first brick building erected in the city was that now occupied by the Commercial National Bank, corner Main and Pine streets, and was built by H. Kahn.

As near as we can discover the first oil well drilled in McKean county was in April, 1866, when oil was found on the Beckwith farm, one mile west of Smithport

The fire which destroyed the old Academy of Music, originating in the Sawyer House, and in which James Wilson was burned to death, occurred on April 3, 1880.

Bradford's great oil fire, which destroyed over $90,000 of property, occurred on June 13, 1876, caused by lightning striking the Olmstead well on the Sandford farm.

The first depot built in Bradford was by the Erie Railroad, and was located on Mechanic street, where Woodbury's Bottling Works now stand. This was in 1864.

The first murder committed in Bradford was that of Major Ashton, a colored man, August 23, 1883. Geo. Gordon, another colored man was charged with the murder.

Company C, Sixeeenth Regiment, left Bradford for the scene of the famous Homestead strike on Monday, July 11. 1892, and were in service until October 14, of the same year.

In 1861 several drillers commenced operations on the Tuna and placed a sign on their derrick bearing the inscription, "Oil, Hell or China." The venture did not prove a success, as neither "Oil, Hell or China," was discovered.

John F. Melvin, father of C. C. and Thos. J. Melvin and Mrs. C. H. Foster and Mrs. Loyal Ward, was married to Miss Lucretia Farr, a daughter of Isaac Farr, on July 12, 1828. This is supposed to have been the first wedding in the valley.

In 1847 Sabinas Walker applied for a license to sell liquor. Walker was the first liquor dealer in the valley. He was the landlord of the old Farmers' Hotel which is still a landmark at the corner of East Main street and Kendall avenue.

Albert DeGolier made his entrance into the valley in 1836, mounted on the back of an old farm horse, along with Mrs. Edson, coming from Smethport. The road they journeyed over was nothing more than a cow path, and at the time covered with snow.

The Tuna Valley Bank was established in 1875, by Whitney & Wheeler, and owing to the panic of 1884 was forced to close its doors. The bank declared the final dividend, which was paid to creditors with interest, in February, 1886. The only losers being the projectors.

In 1853 a company was organized in Buffalo, N. Y., to build a railroad from that city to Bradford, and through to Pittsburg. The road was to be known as the Buffalo, Bradford & Pittsburg Railway. Considerable work was done at several points along the proposed route, but finally the project fell through.

On May 5, 1895, word was received from Glen Hazel to send assistance as a big lumber mills fire was raging. A delegation of the fire department including the "Emery" steamer, in charge of Chief McAllister responded. The mill owners generously donated $325 to the boys for their valuable assistance.

About the first menton of oil was in 440 B. C., by Herodotus, in writing of the black oil of Anderrica. In 1867 oil was discovered by a French missionary, Pere Joseph De la Roche, who called the Cuba oil spring in Allegany, just over the New York line, La Fontaine de bituma.

One of the most exciting days in Bradford was in May, 1879, when news was received that Hon. Lewis Emery, Jr., had been assaulted by Senator Elliott, of Philadelphia, on the floor of the Senate. The cause of the trouble was the opposition of Mr. Emery to a bill taxing rigs and oil. An indignation meeting was held in the Oil Exchange and the Senator's stand in the matter endorsed.

The attempted robbery of the Bradford National Bank occurred on March 6, 1888. Geo. A. Kimball, wearing a mask over his face, entered the bank and leaping over the railing, shot Cashier Tomlinson, and seizing about $600, escaped to the street, pursued by a

large crowd. Seeing he could not escape he turned
and fatally shot Louis Bleich, then placing the weapon
to his own head he fired and died almost instantly.

The burning of the business blocks on the corner of
Main and Mechanic streets, opposite public square, and
which extended from the Conneely Hotel along
Mechanic and around on Main street to Malter Hall,
occurred on January 13, 1895 It was at this fire that
John Crosby, of the Potter Hose Co., contracted the
cold which finally resulted in his death. It was a ter-
ribly cold and stormy Sunday morning, the thermom-
eter registering 14 degrees below zero.

The Bradford Postoffice is considered a rich plum
and at every change of administration a dozen or more
applicants are after it. It is the distributing station for
a large section of country, and many towns, such as
Olean, Eldred and Smethport, report to this office. But
a few old citizens remember the Bradford postoffice
when it was not so pretentious. Sixty years ago the
postoffice consisted of a five-pound raisin box, which
was kept under a bed in William Fisher's house. When
a man called for his mail Fisher, who was postmaster,
would pull out the box, adjust his eye glasses, and in-
spect the bundle it contained.

NEWSPAPERS OF BRADFORD.

The Bradford Miner was first issued on March 12, 1858, by
Sam C. Crane. Six months later he was succeeded
by Daniel Kingsbury, J. K. Haffey and others. The
paper was moved to Smethport in 1863, where it is
still published under the title of the McKean County
Miner by Burt Olson.

The New Era was founded at Bradford in 1875 by J. K.
Haffey as a semi-weekly newspaper. Six months
later it was sold to Ferrin & Weber. On October 29,
1877, the name of the paper was changed to The
Bradford Era and was issued from the office of Weber,
Ferrin & Parsons. In 1879 Longwell, Jordan & Co.
purchased the plant and later Wm. F. Jordan became
the publisher and continued the work until 1886,
when the Era Publishing Co. was formed with P. C.
Boyle as manager. This company now issues a daily
and weekly edition.

The Daily Breeze was established in the fall of 1878 by
David Armstrong for a stock company. Early in
1879 the publishers of the Breeze purchased the opposition Era office, when the Breeze was discontinued
and under a reorganized management was merged
into the Era.

The Bradford Sunday Herald was issued August 4, 1878, by
the Herald Company in the interests of the Labor
Party and Greenback Money.

The Sunday News was established April 15, 1879, by Butler
Bros., who published the paper up to November, 1883,
when the late P. H. Linderman purchased the plant

and continued publication until 1895. The last issue was on March 17, St. Patrick's Day.

The Daily Blaze was established by David Armstrong in April, 1879, at the corner of Newell avenue and Webster street, adjoining the old Academy of Music. The Blaze flickered out after three or four months of brilliancy.

The Star was established in 1879 by Eben Brewer as an evening journal. Late that year the office became the property of F. N. Farrer and A. J. Carr. In May 1880 H. F. Barbour purchased Mr. Carr's interest, and in the same year sold to R. B. Stone. In 1883 the paper became the property of Geo. E. Allen & Co, who conducted it until May, 1884. Then Mr. Barbour again became half owner and editor. In June, 1885, the Star Publishing Company was incorporated with **H.** F. Barbour, president, and R. E. Whiteley, secretary and treasurer, and in October of the same year the office was moved from Pine street to its present quarters in the Producers' Exchange. At the death of Mr. Barbour Hon. F. S. Johnson, administrator, succeeded to the management and became president of the company which position he filled up to the time of his death. Mr. R. B. Stone was next elected president and still acts in that capacity. Mr. Stone's connection with the paper has been somehow continuous since its foundation.

The Petroleum Age was first issued December, 1882, by W. J. McCullough and A. J. Carr. In August, 1883, Mr. A. L. Snell purchased the Petroleum Age, with J. C. McMullen and W. C. Armor as partners. On December 1, 1887, Mr. Snell and Mr. Armor sold their interests to Mr. McMullen who continued the publication until his death.

The Sunday Morning was established in 1882. Phil J. Welch was editor, Benzinger & Edwards. proprietors. The paper lived but a short time, its last issue containing Walt Whitman's poem, "Leaves of Grass." This number was sold for one dollar per copy.

The Sunday Mail was established by A. J. Carr in 1881, and was absorbed by the Star in 1884.

The Evening Call was first issued in November of 1885, and ceased publication the following month.

The Daily Oil News was issued October 3, 1887, by J. C. McMullen and E. A. Bradshaw, and continued until June 1888.

The Evening Record was started in 1890 by Lewis Fmery, Jr. A few years later several other independent oil men became interested in the paper, but there was no actual organization formed. The paper is now published by the Record company.

The Sunday Herald was established in February, 1895, by D. W. Lerch and W. L. Cooper. In February, 1896, Mr Cooper assumed proprietorship. In the summer of the present year the paper was purchased by Laughlin, Murray & Co., but in October last the paper reveverted back to Mr. Cooper who still continues its publication.

The Sunday Post was first issued on August 25, 1895, by Edward F. McIntyre and George O. Slone, who conducted this journal until February , 1897, when the partnership was dissolved, George O. Slone becoming manager and Joseph F. Robinson city editor. Mr. Slone still continues the publication.

The Penny Press was first issued on Thursday, May 21, 1896, F. M. McDonnell being editor and proprietor. In October of the same year Commodore P. H. Linderman became associated with The Press, as business manager and editor, and continued in this capacity until the illness which resulted in his death on June 20, 1897. On April 30, 1897. Mr. R. E. Murphy purchased a half interest in The Press and under the firm name of McDonnell & Murphy the paper was continued until July 16, that being the date of the last issue.

BRADFORD OF TO-DAY.

FACTS ABOUT BRADFORD.

The city is lighted by 107 arc lights.

There are in this city 159 fire hydrants.

The population of Bradford is over 18,000.

Bradford is the metropolis of the oil country.

There are eighteen miles of sewers in the city.

The area covered by the city is about 1460 acres.

Bradford has two wooden and seven iron bridges.

There are over thirty miles of water line in Bradford.

The population of Bradford increased 16,000 in twenty years.

There is four and one-half miles of street railway in the city.

The altitude of Main street is about 1450 feet above the level of the sea.

There are seven and one-tenth miles of paved streets in Bradford and twelve and five-tenths miles unpaved.

POINTS OF INTEREST.

The Wagner Opera House.—Corner Main and Chambers Sts.

Foster Brook Park.—A very popular picnic grounds on O. R. C. & B. St. Ry.

The Great Kinzua Viaduct.—Seventeen miles south of the city. Heighth, 301 feet; length, 2,069 feet. Erected by the Erie railroad in 1882.

Bradford Free Library.—Over 6 and 8 Congress street. The reading room is free to all, and is open week days from 9:30 to 10 p. m. Sunday 9:30 a. m. to 6 p. m.

Clarkdale.—A summer resort about two miles from the St. James Hotel, on line of Bradford street railway. Free vaudeville entertainments afternoons and evenings during the summer months.

Riverside Park. - A picturesque spot on the banks of the Allegheny, nine miles north of the city, on Erie, B. R. & P. and W. N. Y. & P. railways. Good hotel accommodations. Dancing pavilion. Boating and bathing. Under the control of Ed. Sutherland.

Woodbury's Skating Rink.—An ice rink located in the rear of 43 Mechanic street, 125x200 feet. A comfortable sitting room is attached with glass front facing on the ice, where one can rest, or enjoy the pleasant warmth. A most enjoyable resort during the winter months.

Rock City.—Thousands visit this place yearly, many traveling hundreds of miles to view one of the grandest works of nature. The scene is one of indescribable wildness and magnificence, many of the rocks being of such magnitude as to impress the beholder with a feeling of awe as well as admiration. Numerous moss-grown passages abound, and in the summer months the air is delightfully cool. Rock City is situated twelve miles from Bradford on the line of the Olean, Rock City and Bradford Electric railway, in New York state, and six miles from Olean, N. Y. A handsome new hotel, "The Bon Air," has recently been erected, and is probably one of the most complete summer hotels to be found in this section. It is built on solid rock, and the view from the veranda is magnificent. Allegany, five miles away, is one of the picturesque views. The city stands 2,500 feet above the level of the sea, and the climate is said to be unsurpassed for those who are afflicted with asthma or hay fever. The hotel will accommodate a large number of guests. Mr. F. P. Holley, of the Riddell house, Bradford, is proprietor of "The Bon Air."

BRADFORD'S WATER SUPPLY.

The Bradford Water Works Company was originally organized in 1877. In 1879 the company sold the plant to the city of Bradford The success of the city as a manager in this department is undisputable. At the present time we have a source of supply from six artesian wells and water sheds of 12,000 acres. The capacity of the reservoirs is thirty-five million gallons, situated five miles west of the city, and at a height of two hundred and thirty-five feet above the city. The mode of supplying the mains is by gravity. The average pressure is ninety pounds.

CHILDREN'S AID SOCIETY.

The Children's Aid Society was organized in June, 1886, with the following officers: Mrs. L. Emery, Jr., Pres.; Mrs. C. H. Foster, First Vice Pres.; Mrs. A. C.

14

Scott, Second Vice Pres ; Miss C. McBurney, Sec'y, and Mrs. G. Chapman Jones, Treas. The organization is one of which little is heard. Those who have charge of the work in hand have never sought praise or notoriety. Nevertheless the society has done more for the poor and needy of the city of Bradford than is generally known and has brought brightness and cheer to many a fatherless home in times when sickness or loss of work has brou ght poverty and despair. The present officers of the society are Mrs L. Emery, Jr., Pres.; Mrs. R B. Stone, First , ice Pres.: Mrs. Enos. Parsons, Second Vice Pres : Miss Carrie McBurney, Sec'y, and Mrs. C. L. Wheeler, Jr., Treas.

COMPANY C, SIXTEENTH REGIMENT, N. G. P.

Company C completed enrollment and was mustered into service December 23, 1880, as Company C, Seventeenth regiment. They attended their first encampment at Braddock, Pa., in the summer of 1881. After this encampment the Seventeenth regiment was mustered out of service and Company C was assigned to the Sixteenth regiment. The first commissioned officers of the company were: J. C. Fox, captain: Thomas Conneely, first lieutenant, and A. McAlpin, second lieutenant. The present commissioned officers are: A. D. Burns, captain: William J. Bovaird, first lieutenant: Lester H. Simons, second lieutenant. The regimental staff officers are: Major James Johnston. surgeon; Lieutenant Thomas Conneely, inspector rifle practice; Lieutenant Delevan Emery, regimental adjutant; John E. Fennerty, regimental sergeant major. Armory in Producers' exchange.

BRADFORD LIBRARY ASSOCIATION.

The Bradford Library Association was organized in the early days of the oil excitement in Bradford. It was incorporated under charter dated May 19, 1879. In June of this same year they purchased the present lot upon which stands the library building. The library has been added to from time to time until at present it contains over 2,500 volumes of the best literature of the day. The Reading Room is supplied with all the periodicals and all the newspapers and is free to everyone. The Library is under the management of nine directors, who are elected by the stockholders. The present board consists of: T. J. Powers, pres.; R. J. Straight, vice-pres.; E. V. Cody, sec'y; John Ley, treas. C. L. Wheeler, A. M. Mayer, Mrs. L. E. Hamsher, Mrs. L. Emery, Jr., and Miss Carrie McBurney, directors. The librarian is Miss M. C. Gunn. The Library is located over 6 and 8 Congress street.

BRADFORD'S HOSPITAL.

The Bradford Hospital was incorporated July 14, 1885, and opened May 10, 1887. The buildings and grounds are situated on Pleasant street extension, between Bennett and Bennett Brooks roads. The officers of this institution consist of R. B. Stone, Pres.; T. J. Powers, Vice Pres.; Geo. H. Potter, Sec'y. J. C. Greenewald, D. O'Donnell, Geo. H. Potter, T. J. Powers, Dr. C. D. Buss, R. B. Stone, A. D. Sloan, Dr. Jas. Johnston and John Ley, Trustees. The executive committee consists of J. C. Greenewald, Dr. C. D. Russ and Geo. H. Potter. Attending physicians are Drs. H. A. Canfield, H, J. Nichols, A. Grace White, F. W. Winger, W. J. Russell, J. B. Stewart, S. B. Dorn, Jas. Johnston, J. C. Walker, Adelaide M. Griffin, S. H. Haines, and Dr. C. D. Buss, eye and ear specialist. The advisory board consists of Drs. C. S. Hubbard, A. M. Straight and Geo. E. Benninghoff. Geo. H. Potter, Supt. Alice M. Badger, Matron.

BRADFORD FIRE DEPARTMENT.

The first step toward the organization of a Fire Department was the formation of the F. S. Johnson Hose Company on August 2, 1877. The first struggle was at the burning of the Bradford House in May, 1878. This was the second Bradford House destroyed by fire. The next organization was the Era Hook and Ladder Co., which was the result principally of the efforts of Mr. J. L. Andrews, to whom much credit is due for the fame which the Bradford Fire Department has earned. The following list of the different companies will give the balance of the facts as each company follows in line, in the order of their organization, giving the present officers:

Bradford Fire Department Officials.—J. L. Andrews, Pres.; John Meeker, Vice Pres.; Frank Greer, Sec.; J. C. Greenewald, Treas.; Burt McAllister, Chief Engineer; Wm. Toy, First Assistant; C. J. Flick, Second Assistant.

F. S. Johnson Hose Co.—Organized August 2, 1877. Incorporated March 7, 1881. M. Cohn, Pres.; C. B. Willie, Vice Pres.; Geo. Leipold, Sec.; J. B. Fox, Treas.; B. McAllister, W. C. Maxwell, John Calahan, Trustees; W. C. Maxwell, Foreman; Fitz Miles, First Assistant; Wm. Winger, Second Assistant. Headquarters, St. James Place.

Era Hook and Ladder Co.—Organized August 19, 1878. J. L. Andrews, Pres.; F. E. Bradley, Vice Pres.; Robert Howard, Sec'y; R. L. Edgett, Treas.; C. F. Genthner. M. P. Oliver, F. E. Bradley, Trustees; E. A. Hamilton, Foreman; M. P. Oliver, First Asst.; S. C. Avers Second Asst. Headquarters Pine street.

Citizens' Hose Co. (Chemical Engine.)—Organized November 27, 1878. J. C. Greenwald, Pres.; T. A. Flagg, Vice Pres.; Wm. Urquhart, Treas.; Frank Marks, Fin Sec'y; Henry King, Rec. Sec'y; H. Rowan, Geo. Sackrand, Harry Hulme, Trustees; J. W. Banes. Foreman; Benjamin Sackrand, Asst. Headquarters 19 Kennedy street.

Cornen Hose Co. (Independent).—F. A. Meldrum, Pres.; A. Haggerty, Treas.; O. F. Spencer, C. H. Fox

16

R. A. DEMPSEY, MANAGER.   C. G. DEMPSEY.
T. B. DEMPSEY.   H. DEMPSEY.

—

Rock Glycerine Company,

MANUFACTURERS OF THE

Celebrated Nonpareil Powder

· AND ALL GRADES OF

Dynamite and Torpedoes

For Oil and Artesian Wells.

❧

DEALERS IN

BLACK POWDER

AND

BLASTING SUPPLIES.

❧

MAIN OFFICE:

46 Main Street, Bradford, Pa,

❧

Correspondence solicited and promptly and
cheerfully answered.

A. F. DANILSON & CO.

Fire

Insurance

No. 1 Congress St.

........●●●........

TELEPHONE 125.

George Reedy, Trustees; F. A. Greer, Foreman: M. Seeley, First Asst.: John Donohue, Second Asst. Headquarters East Main street.

Central Hose Co., Independent. Organized September, 1885, incorporated February, 1894. W. D. Singleton. Pres.; J. P. Flannigan, Sec'y: F. E. Durfev. Tres.: J. E. Ward, Foreman: J. H. Lohner, Firt Asst.; F. L. Pitkin, Second Asst. Headquarters cor. Boylston and Davis.

Geo. H. Potter Hose Co., Ind. Organized in August, 1891. B. Brown, Pres.: E. J. Riley, Sec'y: M. F. Flaherty, Treas.; John Costello, Foreman: Frank Brown, First Asst.; A. Ward, Second Asst. Headquarters cor. Pleasant and Centre.

Liberty Hose Co., Independent. Organized October 10, 1892. W. H. Shaw, Pres., C. Colligan, Vice Pres.; W. H. Griffith, Treas.; Thos. Sullivan, Rec. Sec.; C. V. Fisher, Fin. Sec'y: Wm. Stewart, R. French, B. Fizzell, Trustees: J. Dougherty. Foreman: J. McCord, Asst. Headquarters, High street.

Fire Police.—Organized August 4, 1896. M. F. Flaherty, Pres.: Frank Marks, Vice Pres.; Frank Snakard, Sec'y: Chas. Green, Treas.; C. F. Genthner, Cyrus Krepps, E. J. McGaughey, Trustees: C. C. Kimball, Capt.; C. F. Genthner, First Lieut.; E. J. McGaughey, Second Lieut. Headquarters Armory Hall, Corydon street.

Fire Engines.—"L. Emery, Jr." and "City of Bradford."

The Weaver Hose Co. This company while not a member of the department are often called upon and render valuable assistance. It is composed of the employes of the firm of Emery & Weaver.

LODGES AND SOCIETIES.

Afro=American League.—Bradford Branch. Organized April, 1897.

Ancient Order United Workmen.—Tunungwant Lodge, No. 11. Organized June 1, 1877. Meets at Exchange Lyceum Hall.

Benevolent Protective Order Elks.—Bradford Lodge, 234. Organized 1892. Meets in Masonic Hall.

Bradford Typographical Union, No. 185.—Organized May 30, 1880. Meets Malta Hall.

Bradford Council, Royal Templars of Temperance.—Meets at W. G T. U. Hall.

Bradford Home Mission.—Organized March 19, 1897. Meets at 17 Chestnut.

Brotherhood of Locomotive Engineers.—Bradford Division, No. 280. Organized November 14, 1894. Meets in Malta Hall.

Brotherhood Railroad Trainmen.—Bradford Lodge, No. 228. Organized July 10, 1886. Meets at Odd Fellows Hall.

Catholic Benevo ent Legion.—Meets at St. Bernard's Hall.

Catholic Mutual Benefit Association.—Branch 13. Organized April 16, 1879. Meets at St. Bernard's Hall.

Chevre Bikur Cholin Relief Association.—Meets at Malta Hall.

Central Labor Union.—Meets at Central Labor Union Hall.

Empire Knights of Relief.—Meet at 4 Boylston street.

Home Circle.—Tuna Valley Council, No. 70. Organized October 8, 1883. Meets at G. A. R. Hall.

Independent Order Foresters.—Gourt Valiant, No. 351. Meets at Malta Hall.

Independent Order Odd Fellows.—McKean Encampment, No. 266. Organized June 18, 1884. Meets at Odd Fellows Hall.

Independent Order Sons of Benjamin.—Don Arbarbanel Lodge, No. 58. Organized April 20, 1884. Meets at Malta Hall.

Junior Order United American Mechanics.—Bradford Branch, No. 309. Meets at Malta Hall.

Knights of Honor.—Osmer Lodge, No. 2365. Organized February 15, 1881. Meets room 4, cor. Main and Congress.

Knights and Ladies of Honor.—L. B. Lockard, Supreme Protector, Whitney Place. Ascension Lodge, No. 1345. Organized 18 9. Bradford Lodge No. 1111. Organized December 10, 1885. Meets G. A. R. Hall.

Knights of Labor.—Bradford Assembly, No. 5405. Meets Central Labor Union Hall.

Knights of Pythias.—Tuna Valley Lodge, No. 453. Meets at Producers' Exchange.

Knights of St. John and Malta.—Bradford Encampent, No. 56. · Organized September 2, 1885. Meets at Malta Hall.

Knights of S. F. I.—Lodge No. 187. Meets at Exchange Lyceum Hall.

Knights of the Maccabees. Bradford Tent, No. 4. Organized May 4, 1884 Meets at Odd Fellows' Hall.

Ladies of the Maccabees.—Crystal Hive, No 5; organized December 3, 1892. Meets at Newell Hall. Clover Hive, No 19; organized April 14, 1893. Meets at Newell Hall. Pearl Hive No. 9. Meets at A. O. U. W. Hall.

Ladies' Catholic Benevolent Association—Meets at St Bernard's Hall.

Masonic.—Bradford Chapter, No. 260, R A. M; constituted September 6, 1880 Bradford Council, No. 43, R and S M.; chartered February 15, 1888. Trinity Commandery, No. 58, K. T.; constituted May 9, 1881. Union Lodge, No. 334, F. and A. M.; instituted March 7, 1859. Meets at Masonic Temple.

National Association Letter Carriers.—Branch 293. Organized January 15, 1891. Meets at 1 Chautauqua Place.

Order Golden Chain.—Bradford Lodge, No. 5. Instituted October 7, 1885. Meets at Exchange Lyceum Hall.

Order of Railway Conductors.—Bradford Division, No. 200.

Organized October 3, 1886. Meets at Odd Fellows Hall

Protected Home Circle.—Bradford Circle, No. 68. Meets at Producers' Exchange Hall.

Retail Clerks' Union.—Meets in Producers' Exchange Hall.

The Eclectic Assembly.—Supreme Prest.; M. S. Van Every; Supreme Vice-prest., L. E. Hamsher; Supreme Sec., M. G. Raub; Supreme Treas., C. W. Dennis; Ass't. Sec., Miss Blanche Custer. Supreme office, Room 1 DuBois Block, 99 Main street. Supreme Council. organized January 3, 1893. Bradford Council No. 1, meets at Newell Hall.

Veterans' Legion.—Meets at 1 Chautauqua Place.

Woman's Christian Temperance Union.—Organized October 17, 1889. Meets at W. C. T. U. Hall.

Young Men's Christian Association.—Free reading room, library and gymnasium. 19-21 Congress.

CHURCHES.

African Methodist Episcopal.—Rev. Charles A. McGee, pastor. Services, 11 a. m. and 7:30 p. m. Cor. Mechanic and Bank.

Church of Eternal Hope (Universalist).—Rev. M. H. Houghton, pastor. Services, 11 a. m. and 7:30 p. m. Cor. Mechanic and Corydon.

East Bradford Presbyterian.—Rev. George Storner, pastor. Services, 11 a. m. and 7:30 p. m. 4-6 Church.

First Baptist.—Rev. William T. C. Hanna, pastor. Services, 10:30 a. m. and 7:30 p. m. Cor. Congress and Corydon.

First Methodist.—Rev. Melville R. Webster, pastor. Services 10:30 a. m. and 7:30 p. m. Cor. Corydon and Chambers.

Free Methodist.—Rev. Francis Cox, pastor. Services, 11 a. a. m. and 7:30 p. m. Pleasant, near Jackson Ave.

First Presbyterian.—Rev. George M. Hickman, pastor. Services, 10:30 a. m. and 7:30 p. m. Corydon, opposite Chambers.

Kendall Methodist Episcopal.—Rev. B. R. Germer, pastor. Services, 11 a. m. and 7:30 p. m. 369-371 East Main.

Orthodox Hebrew.—Rev. Isaac Slick, pastor. Services, first Sunday of every month.

St. Bernard's Roman Catholic.—Rev. William Coonan, pastor. Services: masses, 7:30, 9 and 10:30 a. m.; vespers and benediction, 7:30 p. m. Sunday. Morning mission, week days, 7:30. Corydon, near Webster.

Swedish Lutheran.—Rev. Peter S. Miller, pastor. Services, 10 a. m. and 7:30 p. m. Cor. Mechanic and Walker Ave.

Temple Beth-Zion.—Rev. Louis G. Reynolds, rabbi. Services, Friday evening 7:30, Saturday morning 10, 211 Mechanic.

The Church of the Ascension.—Rev. A. R. Keiffer, rector. Services, Sunday, 8 and 10:40 a. m., 7:45 p. m. Wednesday evening, 7:30. Chautauqua place, near Bushnell.

The Spiritualist.—Rev. Samuel Weil, pastor. Service, Sunday, 3:30 p. m. 1 Chautauqua place.

United Brethren.—Rev. O. J. Gage, pastor. Services, Sunday, 11 a. m. and 8 p. m. Prayer meeting Wednesday, 8 p. m Cor. Boylston and Kennedy.

PUBLIC SCHOOLS.

High School.—Congress st., cor. Tibbitts ave.

Second Ward School.—Congress st., cor. Elm.

Third Ward School.—(Two buildings.) School st., cor. Centre.

Fourth Ward School.—Jackson ave., below Kennedy,

Fifth Ward School.—Elm st.. cor. avenue B.

Sixth Ward School.—179-189 Kendall ave.

THEATRES AND PUBLIC HALLS.

Wagner Opera House.—M. W. Wagner, propr.; F. W. Wagner, mgr. 52-54 Main, cor. Chambers.

Exchange Lyceum.—J. B. Steele, mgr., 35 Main.

K. O. T. M. Hall.—M. B. Delmage, chairman board of trustees. East Bradford. Office, 425 East Main. Hall, 476 East Main.

Pompelon Hall.—Public Square.

Orpheus Hall.—W. R. Weaver, mgr., 41 Main. Tel. 120. 45-47-49 Boylston.

G. A. R. Hall.—Producers' Exchange, Public Square.

St. Bernard's Hall.—Corydon, near Webster.

Central Labor Union Hall.—Railroad, near Erie depot.

Epworth Hall.—373 E. Main.

Odd Fellows Hall.—95 Main.

Exchange Lyceum Hall.—35 Main.

Malta Hall.—11 Main.

Masonic Temple.—73-75 Main.

A. O. U. W. Hall.—412 East Main.

Newell Hall.—Corner Main and Webster.

CEMETERIES.

Oak Hill Cemetery Association.—P. L. Webster, Pres.; D. H. Jack, Vice Pres.; F. M. Webster, Sec'y and Treas. Located on East Main. Office 37 Corydon. Tel. 130-B.

St. Bernards Cemetery.—Located on Washington. street Extension.

Jewish Cemetery.—Located on Washington.

CLUBS.

Bradford Shooting Club.—Organized 1880.

Elite Club.—Organized 1896.

Merchants' Club.—Organized October 3, 1985.

Pompelon Club.—Organized January, 1889.

Scandia Club.—Organized November 9, 1894.

Schubert Club.—Organized February, 1896.

Womans' Literary Club.—Organized 1888.

McKean County Press Association.—Organized 1896.

GRAND ARMY REPUBLIC.

John S. Melvin Post, No. 141.—Department of Pennsylvania. Organized 1881. Meets in G. A. R. Hall, Producers' Exchange, Public Square.

DRIVING PARK.

Bradford Driving Park and Fair Association.—A. C. Hawkins, Pres.; W. R. Weaver, Sec'y. 41 Main. Tel. 120. The park is located at head of Congress Extension.

COMPANY C FOOTBALL TEAM.

Bradford's Football Team was organized in 1896 by members of Company C. The wonderful record made by the team during the season of '97 is worthy of mention. We append the season's record of games played. The present members of the team are: Lester H. Simons, manager; John Lavens, captain; W. C. Stuart, coach; John Miskel, Joe Robinson. Herbert Straight, Dave Stewart, Ralph Coffin, James Lindsey, Jr., Will Bannon, John Leonard, Frank Costello, Harry Kerstetter, Tracy Rider, Ed Knight, Shirley Dodge, Pat Purcell, Harry Douglas, John Ward, Charles McAleer.

The following is the record of games played during the season of '97' resulting in every instance in victory for the home team:

September 25....Fredonia.....................at Bradford......74-0·
October   2........Jamestown..................at Bradford......32-0
October   6........Batavia......................at Bradford......78-0.
October   9........Corry ....at Bradford......40-0
October 16........All Buffalo.......... ......at Buffalo.........18-0
October 26........Altoona-DuBois ....at Bradford......12-0
October 30........Lancaster...................at Bradford......49-0
November 6....Elmira......................at Bradford...... 6-0
November 13....Tonawanda.................at Tonawanda. 4-0
November 20....Rochester Y. M. C. A...at Bradford......65-0
November 25....University of Niagara..at Bradford......10-0

PUBLIC TELEPHONE STATIONS.

At Telephone Exchange, 53 Main street.
At St. James Hotel, 112 Mechanic street.
At Riddell House, 121 Main Street.
At C. N. Pfohl, 55 Main street.
At John Calhoun & Son, 412 East Main street.

THE CITY GOVERNMENT.

THE NEW CITY HALL.

The New City Hall, which is now in process of erection on the corner of Kennedy and Boylston streets. The cost of the structure will exceed $30,000, and when completed it will be one of the finest buildings in the city.

CITY OFFICIALS.

MAYOR.—Geo. C. Fagnan.

CITY SOLICTOR.—Fred P. Schoonmaker.

CITY TREASURER.—Archie McLean.

CITY CONTROLLER.—A. D. Sloan.

CITY CLERK.—James A. Lindsey.

CITY ENGINEER.—P. B. Winfree.

ASSISTANT CITY ENGINEER.—A. F. Bannon, Jr.

STREET COMMISSIONER.—James Anglun.

POLICE JUSTICE.—J. S. Barlow.

CHIEF OF POLICE.—M. Ruddy.

PATROLMEN.—P. F. Scully, C. L. Foust, M. C. Bayne, Fred Willey and Richard Cowan.

CONSTABLES.—First Ward, Thos. Osborne; Second Ward, Geo. R. Gibbons; Third Ward, Thos. J. Fennerty; Fourth Ward, Chas. A. Spreter; Fifth Ward, W. W. Tadder; Sixth Ward, M. F. King.

ALDERMEN.—First Ward, J. S. Barlow; Second Ward, Geo. E. Thomas; Third Ward, C. C. Donoghue; Fourth Ward, L. F. Egbert; Sixth Ward, Capt. Wm. Dobie.

CITY ASSESSORS.—Geo. P. Booth, M. G. Raub, Jos. H. Bovaird.

COUNTY ASSESSORS.—First Ward, Thos. Osborne; Second Ward. Geo. E. Thomas; Third Ward, Thos. J. Fennerty: Fourth Ward, Loyal Ward; Fifth Ward, Eugene Williams, Sixth Ward, G. M. Rathbon.

TAX COLLECTORS.—F. W. Hastings, Jr., State and County. R. L. McCafferty and Mr. Wheeler, City and School.

COUNCILS.

SELECT BRANCH.—First Ward, J. J. Cole; Second Ward, C. V. Merrick: Third Ward, M. F. Flaherty; Fourth Ward, I. G. Howe; Fifth Ward, Wm. H. Shaw; Sixth Ward, Dr. D. E. Ash. I. G. Howe, President; P. N. McCarty, Clerk.

COMMON BRANCH.—First Ward, Cyrus Lester, J. H. Burns; Second Ward, S. H. Smith, W. L. Yelton; Third Ward, C. G. Fitzgibbon, S. A. Terrell: Fourth Ward, T. E. McCray, Norman Parker; Fifth Ward, Jas. G. Paul, T. D. Henretty; ...., C. B. Whitehead. Jas. .. Cleary. T. E. McCray, President, Jas. A. Linsey, Clerk.

SELECT STANDING COMMITTEES.

Finance, Tax, Salaries, Appropriations.—Flaherty, Merrick, Cole.

Streets, Sewers, Bridges, Sidewalks, Railroads.—Ash, Cole, Merrick.

City Property, Light, Water.—Merrick, Flaherty, Shaw.

Fire and Police.—Shaw, Ash, Flaherty.

Ordinance, Rules, Printing, Health.—Cole, Shaw, Ash.

COMMON STANDING COMMITTEES.

Finance, Tax, Salaries, Appropriations.—Parker, Paul, Terrell.

Streets, Sewers, Bridges, Sidewalks, Railroads.—Lester, Fitzgibbon, Whitehead.

City Property, Light, Water.—Fitzgibbon, Burns, Yelton.

Fire and Police.—Burns, McCleary, Henretty.

Ordinance, Rules, Printing, Health.—McCleary, Smith, Henretty.

POOR BOARD.

OFFICERS. · Wm. Dobie, Pres.; Bruce Davis, Sec'y.
MEMBERS.—Thos. McDonald, Bruce Davis, J. F. Leonard, M. J. Benjamin, W. H. Leyman, Wm. Dobie.

BOARD OF SCHOOL CONTROL.

W. R. WEAVER, Pres.

B. S. LOVE, Sec'y.

A. D. SLOAN, Controller.

A. McLEAN, Tres.

E. E. MILLER, Supt.

MEMBERS.—A. DeGolier, C. J. Lane, W. R. Weaver, L. C. Blakeslee, T. E. Costello, J. W. Willis, F. A. Fralic, C. D. Buss, D. Armstrong, M. D. Harris, F. O. Hane, M. W. Piper.

STANDING COMMITTEES.

Finance.—Costello, Willis, Fralic.

Text Books, Studies, Grades.—Armstrong, Buss, Blakeslee.

Teachers and Salaries.—DeGolier, Harris, Willis.

Building and Supplies.—Lane, DeGolier, Hane.

Law.—Buss, Costello, Piper.

Library.—Hane, Fralic, Blakeslee.

Rules and Regulations. Harris, Piper, Armstrong.

Board meets first and third Friday of each month.

BOARD OF HEALTH.

DR. C. D. BUSS, President.

JAS. A. LINDSEY, Secretary.

J. FRANKLIN, Health Officer.

BOARD.—Dr. Fred W. Winger, L. B. Waters, C. P. McAllister. Dr. C. D. Buss, E. R. Sherman.

BOARD OF WATER COMMISSIONERS.

T B. Clark, F. D. Wood, J. B. Fox.

S. D. Heffner, Supt.   E. N. Hallock, Sec'y.

COUNTY OFFICIALS.

PRESIDENT JUDGE.—A. G. Olmsted.

ADDITIONAL LAW JUDGE.—T. A. Morrison.

PROTHONOTARY, REGISTER, RECORDER.—G. W. Mitchell.

SHERIFF.—J. F. Davis.

DEPUTY SHERIFF.—W. B. Clarke.

DISTRICT ATTORNEY.—Sheridon Gorton.

TREASURER.—T. B. Clarke.

COMMISSIONERS.—W. A. Young, Lemuel Davis, T. F. Hungiville.

COMMISSIONERS' CLERK.—S. D. Weaver.

AUDITORS.—C. W. Freeman, J. C. Cannon, Jr., A. R. Cory.

JURY COMMISSIONERS.—W. R. Ford, Walter Ostrander.

BRADFORD AS A MANUFACTURING POINT.

——o——

A Few of Its Natural Advantages—Its Railroad Facilities—Cheap Fuel and Water.

Natural gas at a few cents per thousand feet. Its supply practically inexhaustible. We have upwards of forty thousand acres of undeveloped gas territory; we are very saving in its use and the supply should last at least fifty years.

Being practically in the center of the great coal fields of Pennsylvania we can supply coal to the factories at an approximate figure of $1.15 per ton.

Our shipping facilities are of the best. We are on Buffalo rates rates each way. We have six railroads entering the city.

For wood-working factories Bradford offers many advantages, being located in the center of thousands of acres of virgin forests, which should save thousands of dollars in freightage.

Bradford is one of the best location for factories in the iron and steel industry. The iron ore can be delivered at the factory here as cheap as at any of the lake points, and with the use of cheap natural gas for fuel gives Bradford great advantage over other cities.

Bradford is an excellent point for the location of woolen mills, knitting mills and silk factories, wnich require female help. Having none such here at present employing this kind of help it can be readily seen that we could sup ly a few concerns of this kind

For the manufacture of glass we claim superior facilities over any other location in the United States. With natural gas and coal for fuel, low freight rates, and our proximity to the large eastern markets, the western factories cannot compete for the eastern trade, We have at our very doors some of the best glass sand in the United States, which shows over 99 per cent. pure silica. This sand can be had practically without cost, merely the crushing, cartage, and seiving to its proper mesh.

One of the most important industries which we have, and which should be doubled and tripled, is the brick industry. We have without a doubt the finest shales and clays to be found for the manufacture of brick, from the paving brick to the finest of pressed brick. Our brick took the first premium at the World's Fair in 1893, and can be found in some of the largest and most expensive office, store and residence buildings in the United States. Our vitrified brick, which was tested by the United States Ordnance Department at Watervliet Arsenal, Faneuil, Mass., st od an open pressure of twenty-five tons, and is pronounced by experts as the best brick made. Our brick will also take a most excellent enamel and is by experts pronounced superior to the English enameled brick, as well as those made in New Jersey and Canada. The factories that we have at present in this line are exceedingly prosperous and continually increasing their capacity. The field in this line is practically unlimited and the trade could use the output of many more factories making this superior quality of brick.

The Board of Trade and citizens of Bradford are exceedingly enterprising and take great pleasure in furthering the interests of its manufacturing industries. They are liberal in their inducements to get factories to locate in our rapidly growing city and anyone desiring to go into any kind of manufacturing business, or factories that desire a change in location should not lose the opportunity of thoroughly investigating the many and highly important inducements which our thriving city throws open to capital which is seeking investment and location in the manufacturing line. We practically offer free fuel, which is a heavy item to all manufacturing concerns, and with our exceedingly low freight rates, East. West. North and South, our city should grow so fast that within the next ten years we should be known throughout the United States and continent as one of the greatest manufacturing cities in this country. The Board of Trade will be pleased to hear from individuals or firms desiring to change their locations, or parties desiring to start in the manufacturing business and will give them at the present time special inducement to locate in our city. No firm can afford to start a new factory, or change their present location without consulting the Bradford Board of Trade.

MARVELOUS GROWTH OF THE CITY.

From the time when Col. Little selected the present site of Bradford as a more favorable point for a town than either Kendall or Limestone, which was in 1837, calling it Litteton, and up to the present time. there has been a constant growth; naturally slow at first. in those days when railroads were unknown and even wagon roads were scarce and these hardly deserving the name, but gradually, as these obstacles were removed, increasing each year until about 1855 when affairs in this valley took on new life and vigor and for the next few years there was a concerted effort on the part of the business men to boom the town. In 1873 the town became a borough. In 1875 was the real commencement of the wonderful growth of Bradford. It was at this time that Hon Lewis Emery. Jr., struck a large well at Tot Hollow. Then came the "oil excitement" and from that on there has been no lagging in the advancement of all business interests. On January 14, 1879, a city charter was granted. And what a city is Bradford to-day! Elegant brick business blocks are being erected each year. Magnificent homes have sprung up and adorn the residence streets of the city. The streets that are not already paved are being so at a rapid rate, there being now over seven miles, and almost all of vitrified brick. Four railroads making it possible to start on a journey in any direction at almost any hour of the day. Street railway service. And rapidly nearing completion a $30,000 city building. The people are citified in their manners and customs. A stranger in the city observes this at once. The business houses wear a city-like appearance. One of the handsomest streets one could wish to see is Main street at night, each store being brilliantly illuminated and the window displays something that cannot help but attract the eye. The streets thronged with people at any hour of the day and far into the night. And the most sociable people to be found in the world. Bradford gives promise of one day, and that not far away, of being a city of 30,000 population.

BRADFORD BOARD OF TRADE.

The Bradford Board of Trade is a corporation, organized at Bradford, Pa., in 1882, and which was granted a charter and certificate of corporation on December 19, 1882. for the purpose of protecting, fostering and developing the commercial, manufacturing and business interests of the city of Bradford by joint and concerted action. Recently the Grocers' Union joined the organization and a large number of prominent citizens have become members. New life and energy will be infused into the work of the board and a determined effort will be made to bring a number of new industries to Bradford.

A. J EDGETT, President.
F. E. DURFEY, First Vice-President.
GEO. C. FAGNAN, Second Vice-President.
GEO. S. STEWART, Treasurer.
A. DEGOLIER, Secretary.

Directors—A, D. Burns, A. DeGolier, Geo. C. Fagnan, G. C. Greenwald, A. M. Mayer, Geo. S. Stewart, F. E. Durfey, Alex. Watson, E. B. Boylston, A. I. Edgett, C. H. Foster, R. B. Stone, L. W. Oaks, J. M. Sloan, S. H. Smith, M. W. Wagner, C. B. Whitehead.

Headquarters of the board are at No. 1, Congress street. Tel. 125.

GENERAL INFORMATION.

POSTAL INFORMATION.

RATES OF POSTAGE.

First-Class Mail Matter.—Written matter, that is letters, postal cards and all matter wholly or partly in writing, sealed or unsealed, (except manuscript copy accompanyiny proof-sheets, or corrected proof-sheets of the same,) and all matter sealed or otherwise closed against inspection. Rates: Two cents an oun~~ or fraction thereof. Drop letters. wh~~ f~~e delivery is in force, the same. an~ w~~.on not in force, one cent.

Second-Class Mail Matter.—Periodical publication, such as newspapers. and all periodical publications, either for the dissimination of public information, or devoted to literature, science or art, or some special industry, benevolent or fraternal society or order having a bona fide membership of one thousand; formed of printed paper sheets, without board cloth leather or other substantial binding, and having a stated time of publication. Rates: One cent a pound when sent by publishers from office of publication, or one cent for each four ounces or fraction thereof when sent by others.

Third-Class Mail Matter.—Books, circulars, pamphlets and other matter wholly in print, (not included in second-class matter) proof-sheets, corrected proof-sheets, and manuscript copy accompanying the same. Rates: One cent for each two ounces or fractional part thereof.

Fourth-Class Mail Matter.—All matter not embraced in the first, second or third-class, which is not in its form or nature liable to destroy, deface, or otherwise damage the contents of the mail bag, or harm the person of anyone engaged in the postal service. Rates: One cent an ounce or fraction thereof.

GENERAL INFORMATION

The sender of a letter may withdraw it from the post office, either before it has been started on its route, or afterwards and before its delivery at end of destination, upon proof in writing of his authority to do so, as required by the postmaster, and the deposit of a sum sufficient to defray all necessary expenses attached.

Any article of mailable matter bearing a ten-cent special delivery stamp in addition to the required postage, will be entitled to immediate delivery or arrival at destination between the hours of 7 a. m. and 11 p. m., at free delivery offices; or between 7 a. m. and 7 p. m. at any other post office, providing the letter is addressed to a point within the carrier limits or within one mile of postoffice.

The rates of postage to Canada and Mexico, are the same as in the United States, except that sealed packages, other than letters in there ordinary shape and form, are absolutely excluded.

RATES CHARGED FOR MONEY ORDERS.

For Orders for sums not exceeding $ 2.50............ 3 cents
Over $ 2.50 and not exceeding $ 5.00............ 5 cents
Over $ 5.00 and not exceeding $ 10.00............ 8 cents
Over $10.00 and not exceeding $ 20.00............10 cents
Over $20.00 and not exceeding $ 30.00............12 cents
Over $30.00 and not exceeding $ 40.00............15 cents
Over $40.00 and not exceeding $ 50.00............18 cents
Over $50.00 and not exceeding $ 60.00............20 cents
Over $60.00 and not exceeding $ 75.00............25 cents
Over $75.00 and not exceeding $100.00............30 cents

————

ARRIVAL AND DEPARTURE OF MAILS
From Bradford Postoffice.

J. H. OSSENBECK, P. M.   T. E. COSTELLO, Ass't P. M.

Mails Arrive from

Albany, N Y, 7 30 a m and 10 05 p m
Boston, Mass., 6 30, 7 30 and 11 45 a m; 12 20 p m
Binghamton, N Y, 6 30, 7 30 and 11 45 a m
Baltimore, Md. 6 30, 7 30 and 11 45 a m; 8 40 p m
Buffalo, N Y, 7 30 and 11 15 a m; 6 25 and 8 40 p m

Chicago, Ill. 9 25 a m and 6 25 p m
Cincinnati, O, 9 25 a m and 6 25 p m
Cleveland, O, 9 25 a m and 6 25 p m
Canada, 9 25 and 11 15 a m: 6 25 p m
Dunkirk, N Y, 9 25 and 11 15 a m; 6 25 p m
DuBois, Pa, 1 45 and 4 30 p m
Elmira. N Y, 7 30 and 11 45 a m
Eldred, Pa, 4 30 p m
Erie, Pa, 9 25 a m and 6 25 p m
Findlay, O, 9 25 a m and 6 25 p m
Jamestown, N Y, 6 30, 9 25 and 11 45 a m: 6 25 p m
Kane, Pa, 9 30 a m; 1 45 and 6 40 p m
Lima, O, 9 25 a m and 6 25 p m
Meadville, Pa, 9 25 and 11 45 a m; 6 25 p m
Mt Jewett, Pa, 9 30 a m; 1 45 and 4 30 p m
New York City, 6 30, 7 30 and 11 45 a m
Oil City, Pa, 9 25 and 11 45 a m; 6 25 p m
Olean, N Y, 6 30 and 11 47 a m; 6 25 p m
Philadelphia, Pa, 6 30 and 11 45 a m; 1 45 p m   .
Pittsburg, Pa, 9 25 a m; 4 30 and 6 25 p m
Ridgway, Pa, 1 45 and 4 30 p m
Rochester, N Y, 9 25 a m; 12 05, 6 25 and 8 30 p m
St. Louis, Mo, 9 25 a m and 6 25 p m
Salamanca, N Y. 9 25 a m; 12 05 and 6 25 p m
Sistersville, W Va, 9 25 a m: 4 30 and 6 25 p m
Smethport, Pa, 9 30 a m and 6 30 p m
Syracuse, N Y. 6 30. 7 30 and 9 25 a m: 12 05 p m
Titusville, Pa, 9 25 and 11 45 a m; 6 25 p m
Utica, N Y, 6 30, 9 25 a m; 12 10 and 6 25 p m
Warren, Pa, 6 30 a m and 6 25 p m
Washington, D C, 7 30 a m; 12 05 and 1 45 p m
Wheeling, W Va, 9 25 a m and 6 25 p m
Williamsport. Pa, 6 30 and 7 30 a m; 1 45 p m

Mails Close for

Albany, N Y, 7 45. 10 10 a m; 2 30 and 4 45 p m
Boston, Mass, 7 00, 10 10 a m: 1 55, 4 15 and 7 40 p m
Binghamton, N Y, 7 00, 10 10 a m; 4 15 and 7 40 p m
Baltimore, Md, 6 30, 7 05, 10 10 a m; 4 15 and 7 40 p m
Buffalo, N Y, 7 45, 10 10 a m; 1 55, 4 15 and 7 40 p m
Chicago, Ill, 10 10 a m; 1 55, 4 15 and 7 40 p m
Cincinnati, O, 10 10 a m; 1 55, 4 15 and 7 40 p m
Cleveland. O, 10 10 a m; 1 55, 4 15, and 7 40 p m
Canada, 7 45, 10 10 a m; 1 55, 4 15 and 7 40 p m
Dunkirk, N Y, 10 10 a m; 1 55, 4 15, and 7 40 p m
DuBois, Pa, 6 30 a m; 12 15 and 4 00 p m
Elmira, N Y, 7 00, 10 10 a m; 4 15 and 7 40 p m
Eldred, Pa, 7 45 a m; 1 55 and 4 15 p m
Erie, Pa, 10 10 a m; 3 00, 4 15 and 7 40 p m
Findlay, O, 10 10 a m; 1 55, 4 15 and 7 40 p m
Jamestown, N Y, 10 10 a m; 3 00 and 7 40 p m
Kane, Pa, 6 30 a m; 12 15 and 4 p m
Lima, O, 10 10 a m; 1 55, 4 15 and 7 40 p m
Meadville, Pa, 10 10 a m; 3 00 and 7 40 p m
Mt Jewett, Pa, 6 30 a m; 12 15 and 4 15 p m
New York City, 7 05, 10 10 a m; 4 15 and 7 40 p m
Oil City, Pa, 6 00, 10 10 a m; 1 55, 3 00 and 7 40 p m
Olean, N Y, 7 00, 10 10 a m; 1 55, 4 15 and 7 40 p m
Philadelphia, Pa, 7 00, 10 10 a m; 4 00 and 7 40 p m
Pittsburg, Pa, 6 00, 7 05, 10 10 a m and 7 40 p m

29

Ridgway, Pa, 6 30 a m; 12 15 and 4 00 p m
Rochester, N Y, 7 45, 10 10 a m; 1 55, 4 15 and 7 40 p m
St Louis, Mo, 10 10 a m; 1 55 and 7 40 p m
Salamanca, N Y, 10 10 a m; 1 55, 4 15 and 7 40 p m
Sistersville, W Va, 6 00, 7 10, 10 10 a m, and 7 40 p m
Smethport, Pa, 7 00, 7 30 a m; 1 20 and 4 p m
Syracuse, N Y, 7 45, 10 10 a m; 1 55, 4 15 and 7 40 p m
Titusville, Pa, 6 00, 10 10 a m; 3 00 and 7 40 p m
Utica, N Y, 7 45, 10 10 a m; 1 55, 4 15 and 7 40 p m
Warren, Pa, 6 00 a m; 1 20 and 7 40 p m
Washington, D C, 6 00, 7 05, 10 10 a m; 4 00 and 7 30 p m
Wheeling, W Va, 6 00, 7 00 10 10 a m, and 7 40 p m
Williamsport, Pa, 6 00, 7 05 10 10 a m; 4 00 and 7 40 p m.

Stage Routes.

Bradford via Sawyer City, Dallas City, Summit City, Rixford, Duke Center, Pa, and Prentissvale, Pa, to Eldred, arrives 12 noon; leaves at 2 15 p m daily, except Sunday.

Bradford via Derrick City, Goodell, Pa, Knapps Creek and Four Mile, N Y, to Olean leaves daily at 6 a m, returning at 6 p m, except Sunday.

Local Mail.

Between Bradford and Wellsville closes 7 10, 10 40 a m; 4 15 p m. Arrives 7 30, 11 45 a m; 4 12 p m.
Between Bradford and Punxsutawney closes 6 30 a m, 12 15 p m Arrives 1 45, 4 30 p m.
Between Bradford and Rochester closes 1 55 p m. Arrives 12 05 p m.
Between Bradford and Buffalo closes 4 15 p m. Arrives 11 15 a m.
Between Olean and Emporium closes 7 45 a m. Arrives 8 45 p m.
Between Carrollton and Dunkirk closes 10 10 a m and 1 55 p m. Arrives 6 25 p m.
Between Hornellsville and New York closes 7 10, 10 10 a m, 4 15, 7 40 p m. Arrives 7 30 and 11 45 a m.
Between Salamanca and Leavittsburg closes 10 10 a m, 7 40 p m. Arrives 6 30, 11 45 a m; 6 25 p m.
Between Salamanca and Oil City closes 6 a m, 1 55 p m. Arrives 6 25 p m.
Between Olean and Buffalo closes at 7 45 a m, 1 55 p m. Arrives 4 30 p m.

Office Hours.

Money orders and registered letters, 8 a m to 6 p m
General delivery and stamps 8 a m to 8 p m.
Extra collection of mail from letter boxes on business streets, 6 a m and 7 p m.
Business street delivery, 8, 10 30 a m; 1 30 and 7 p m
Resident street delivery, 8 a m, 1 30 p m
Carriers' windows open daily, 7 to 8 p m.
Carriers' windows open Sunday 1 to 2 p m
Sunday's mail for North and West closes 10 10 a m.
Sunday's mail for South and East closes 4 15 p m.

LOCATION OF FIRE ALARM BOXES.

FIRST WARD.

No. 12 Riddell House.
13 Cor Main and Chestnut.
14 St. James Hotel.
15 Cor. Corydon and Bushnell.
16 Cor. Corydon and Webster.
17 Cor. Congress and Corydon.
18 Cor. Boylston and Bishop.

SECOND WARD.

No. 22 Cor. Sherman and Congress Extention.
23 Cor. Congress and Park.
24 Cor. Webster and Elm.
25 Cor. Congress and Kane.
26 Cor. Mechanic and Potter.
27 Cor Congress Extension and Blaisdell ave.
28 Blaisdell Factory.
29 Cor Mechanic and Pike.

THIRD WARD.

No. 31 Terril Bros.' Grocery.
32 Cor. School and Centre.
34 Cor. Washington and Centre.
35 Cor. Summer and Centre.
36 Cor. Pleasant and Bennett.
37 Cor. Centre and Brookline.
38 Cor State and McClellan.
39 Cor. Pleasant and Pearl.

FOURTH WARD.

No. 41 Cor. Foreman and Kennedy.
42 Cor. Kennedy and Jackson ave.
43 Cor. Petrolia and Jackson ave.
44 Walker ave.
45 Hilton, near Watson's mill.
46 Cor. Mechanic and School.
47 Mill street, near Hardwood Factory.
48 Cor. Davis and Miller.
49 Cor. Jackson and Barry aves.

FIFTH WARD.

No. 51 Cor Main and East Main.
52 Cor. High and Elm.
53 East Main, near Oak Hill.
54 High street Extention.
55 Cor. Roberts and North.
56 B., R. & P. R. R. Shops.
57 Cor. Rochester and Oak.

SIXTH WARD.

No. 61 American Hotel.
62 Cor. Kendall and Seward aves.
63 Cor. East Main and Logan.
64 East Main, near Clark Farm.
65 Cor. Rockland and Jerome aves.

FIRE ALARM SIGNALS.

Seven taps of the bell will constitute a general alarm, except the Cornen Hose Co. If Cornen Hose is needed three taps of the bell will be given.

REPUBLICAN COUNTY COMMITTEE,
McKean County, Pennsylvania.

George, W. Mitchell, Chairman.
J. M. McElroy and C. G. Boyd, Secretaries.

EXECUTIVE COMMITTEE:

John P. Melvin, Chairman; Louis Marck, Wesley Beck-with, Albert Peterson, Thomas Potter, C. A. Duke, W. F. Andrews.

COUNTY COMMITTEEMEN:

Annin Township—J. J. McCarey, Turtle Point, Pa.
Bradford City, 1st Ward, 1st District—J. C. Greenewald, Bradford.
Bradford City, 1st Ward, 2d District—J. L. Andrews, Bradford.
Bradford City, 2d Ward, 1st District—John P. Melvin, Bradford.
Bradford City, 2d Ward, 2d District—Louis Marck, Bradford.
Bradford City, 3d Ward—J. B. Rutherford, Bradford.
Bradford City, 4th Ward 1. G. Howe, Bradford.
Bradford City, 5th Ward—E. F. Williams, Bradford.
Bradford City, 6th Ward—J. C. Smith, Bradford.
Bradford Twp., 1st Dist.- E. B. Cloud, CusterCity, Pa.
Bradford Twp., 2d Dist—Griffith Hatfield, Bradford.
Ceres Township—F. B. King, Ceres, N. Y.
Corydon, 1st District—B. D. Tome, Corydon, Pa.
Corydon, 2d District—E. N. Homes, Cornplanter, Pa.
Eldred Boro—A, Ortman, Eldred, Pa.
Eldred Township, C. M. Slack, Eldred, Pa.
Foster Twp., 1st Dist.—Thomas Potter, DerrickCity, Pa.
Foster Twp., 2d Dist.—A. W. Boyd, Sawyer City, Pa.
Hamilton Twp., 1st Dist.—John Logan, Ludlow, Pa.
Hamilton Twp., 2d Dist.—William Campbell, Morrison, Pa
Hamlin Twp., 1st Dist.—George Richards, Hazelhurst, Pa.
Hamlin Township 2d District—Chas. Paulson, Lantz, Pa.
Kane Boro, 1st Ward—C. W. Grout, Kane, Pa.
Kane Boro, 2d Ward—Albert Peterson, Kane, Pa.
Kane Boro, 3d Ward—C. C. Davis. Kane, Pa.
Keating Twp., 1st Dist.—I. S. Reynolds, E. Smethport, Pa.
Keating Twp., 2d Dist.—W. P. Beckwith, Farmers Valley.
Keating Twp., 3d Dist.—J. L. McIntyre, Cyclone, Pa.
Lafayette Twp., 1st Dist.—George E. Beaumont, Jr., Mt. Alton, Pa.
Lafayette Twp., 2d Dist —J. C. Cannon, Jr,, Lewis Run.
Lafayette Twp., 3d Dist.—Quinton Clark, Lafayette, Pa.
Liberty Twp.—W. C. Ostrender, Port Allegheny, Pa.
Mt. Jewett Boro—George K. Wilson, Mt. Jewett, Pa.
Norwich Twp.. 1st Dist.—L. F. Wilcox, Newerf, Pa.
Norwich Twp., 2d Dist.—W. F. Andrews, Gardeau, Pa.
Otto Twp., 1st Dist.—C. A. Duke, Duke Centre, Pa.
Otto Twp., 2d Dist.—R. H. Wissinger, Rixford, Pa
Port Allegany Boro—C. W. Catlin, Port Allegheny. Pa.
Sergeant Twp., 1st Dist.—Geo. G. Wandrum, Clermont, Pa
Sergeant Twp., 2d Dist.—H. H. Varner, Burning Well, Pa.
Smethport Boro—E. M. Kerns, Smethport, Pa.
Wetmore Twp,, 1st Dist.—W. Wilkins, Kanesholm, Pa.
Wetmore Twp., 2d Dist.—James F. Swoop, Kane, Pa.

FIRE, LIFE AND ACCIDENT
INSURANCE.

•••••●●●•••••

The Penn Mutual Life Insurance Co
OF PHILADELPHIA.

Incorporated and commenced business in 1847

It has assets exceeding..........................$ 31,000,000
It has a surplus of more than.............. 3,750,000
It has insurance in force, more than..... 145,000,000
Its premium income is more than......... 6,000,000
Its interest income is more than........... 1,500,000
It has paid families of members over... 22,000,000
It has paid to members themselves...... 23,000,000

It is purely mutual in its organization; that is, the policy holders are the members and they manage the institution in their interest through the trustees and officers selected by them.

Central Accident Insurance Company

Writes the best Policy that has ever been presented to the World.

This company is chartered under the laws of Pennsylvania, the most stringent in the world to-day, compelling the company to put up a sufficient amount of **cash** with the Insurance Department at Harrisburg to secure Policy Holders.

It accumulates in value Five per cent. each year to Policy Holders for Ten years without any extra cost to Policy Holder.

They cover all unprovoked assaults.

They do not deduct weekly indemnity for losses paid during the year.

They do not pro rate their insurance.

Costello Bros. represent this Company for McKean county.

COSTELLO BROS.,
GENERAL AGENTS,

110 Mechanic Street.   'Phone, 224.

H. M. PLAGUE,

DEALER IN

Wines, Liquors and Cigars

WHOLESALE AND RETAIL.

SOLE AGENT FOR THE CELEBRATED

J. H. Cutter and McKean Club Rye Whiskies.

108 MECHANIC STREET.

DEMOCRATIC COUNTY COMMITTEE.
McKean County, Pennsylvania.

F. M. Kelleher, Chairman.

COUNTY COMMITTEE.

Annin Twp.—Charles Wandover, Turtle Point, Pa.
Bradford City, 1st Ward—H. Frank, Bradford, Pa.
Bradford City, 1st Ward—Thomas Osborne, Bradford.
Bradford City, 2d Ward—James Anglun, Bradford.
Bradford City, 2d Ward—P. C. Blaisdell, Bradford.
Bradford City, 3d Ward—F. E. Bradley, Bradford.
Bradford City, 4th Ward—P. T. Lane, Bradford.
Bradford City, 5th Ward—James Paul, Bradford.
Bradford City, 6th Ward—Felix Quinlan, East Bradford.
Bradford Twp., 1st Dist.—N. C. Clark, Bradford.
Bradford Twp., 2d Dist.—C. M. O'Conner, Bradford.
Ceres Twp.—O. P. Coon, Ceres, N. Y.
Corydon Twp., 1st Dist.—C. L. Knapp, Corydon, Pa.
Corydon Twp., 2d Dist.—C. D. Seaman, Cornplanter, Pa.
Eldred Boro—J. P. Shay, Eldred, Pa.
Eldred Twp.—W. M. Brooder, Sartwell, Pa.
Foster Twp., 1st Dist—I. P. Hullitt, Derrick City, Pa.
Foster Twp., 2d Dist.—W. T. Haxton, Sawyer City, Pa.
Hamilton Twp., 1st Dist.—M. T. Smith, Ludlow, Pa.
Hamilton Twp., 2d Dist.—Wm. C. Anderson, Morrison, Pa.
Hamlin Twp., 1st Dist.—S. W. Patterson, Kasson, Pa
Hamlin Twp., 2d Dist.—Frank McCuen, Mt. Jewett, Pa.
Keating Twp., 1st Dist.—Allen Oviatt, Smethport, Pa.
Keating Twp., 2d Dist.—S. H. Elder, Coleville, Pa.
Keating Twp., 3d Dist.—G. T. Latterman, Aiken, Pa.
Kane City, 1st Ward—C. B. Gillis, Kane, Pa.
Kane City, 2d Ward—P. J. Murphy, Kane, Pa.
Kane City, 3d Ward—Ed Stophel, Kane, Pa.
Lafayette Twp., 1st Dist.—J. J. O'Connell. Mt. Alton, Pa,
Lafayette Twp., 2d Dist.—J C. Cannon, Lewis Run, Pa.
Lafayette Twp., 3d Dist. Morris Fenton, Taintors, Pa.
Liberty Twp.—J. K. Moore, Port Allegany, Pa.
Mt. Jewett, Boro—W. J. Kerr, Mt. Jewett, Pa.
Port Allegany Boro—W. H. Keeney, Port Allegany, Pa.
Norwich Twp., 1st Dist.—John Boyer, Colegrove, Pa.
Norwich Twp., 2d Dist.—
Otto Twp., 1st Dist.—John C. Mills, Duke Centre, Pa.
Otto Twp , 2d Dist.—H. T. Breeze, Rixford, Pa.
Sergeant Twp., 1st Dist.—James Maloney, Clermont, Pa.
Sergeant Twp., 2d Dist.—Alex. Shinel, Hutchinson, Pa.
Smethport Boro—D. H. Quinlan, Smethport, Pa.
Wetmore Twp., 1st Dist.—Frank Glatt, Kane, Pa.
Wetmore Twp., 2d Dist.—J. H. Reigel, Kane, Pa.

ANNUAL WATER RATES OF BRADFORD CITY, PA.

Dwellings, one family, first faucet..............$	4 00
" " each additional faucet	60
Hot Water Boiler.....................................	60
Bath Tub, private......................................	1 20
" " each additional..............	60
" public, each.........	3 00
" hotels, each...............................	3 00

Urinals, hotels and blocks, self-acting fau-
cets, each... 2 00
Urinals, one family, self-acting faucets, each 1 00
Water Closets, one family, first seat............ 2 00
Water Closets, one family, each additional
seat... 60
Water Closets, hotel, each seat.................... 2 40
Wash Trays, one family, each part.............. 60
Sprinkler, for season.................................... 5 00
Soda Fountain, with tumbler washers......... 3 60
Beer Pump....................~............................... 5 00
Beer Pump, if used for other purposes, Com-
missioners may require them to take
water by meter at meter rates.
Stables, one plain faucet each, annual......... 1 00
" hose bibs when used as washers...... 3 00 to 12 00
Commissioners may require owners of
stables to take water at meter rates.
Motors, meter rates per 1,000 gallons........... 06
Banks and Stores, first faucet...................... 4 00
"   "   each additional faucet.... 60
Drug Stores, first faucet.............................. 6 00
"   each additional faucet.............. 60
Bakeries, first faucet... .... 6 00
"   each additional faucet.................. 60
Ice Cream Parlors, first faucet...................... 4 00
" , "   each additional faucet... 60
Restaurants, Saloons and Bar Rooms, first
faucet.......... .... 12 00
Restaurants, Saloons and Bar Rooms, each
additional faucet........................... 60
Barber Shop, two chairs............................... 5 00
"   each additional chair.............. 60
Photographers, first operator....................... 5 00
"   each additional operator...... 2 40
Billiard Rooms, first faucet.......................... 7 00
"   each additional faucet......... 60
Boarding Houses, first faucet.................. 4 00 to 12 00
"   each additional faucet..... 60
Printing Offices, first faucet........................ 5 00
"   each additional faucet...... 60
Meat Market, first faucet............................. 5 00
"   each additional faucet............ 60
Fish Market, first faucet.......................... 5 00 to 20 00
"   each additional faucet............ 65
Masonry, Stone, per cubic yard.................... 00
"   Brick, per 1,000 laid..................... 04
"   Plastering, per 100 square yards... 25
All use of water not enumerated in above list to be
rated upon application to Water Board.

MAYORS OF BRADFORD.

The following are the names of the mayors of Bradford,
and their terms of office, from date of incorporation as a
city: James Broder, 1879-80; William F. Jordan, 1881-82,
deceased; James Broder, 1883-84; P. M. Shannon, 1885-86;
R. A. Dempsey, 1887-88; Edward McSweeney, 1889; Loyal
Ward, 1890-91-92; R. A. Dempsey, 1893-94-95; George C.
Fagnan, 1896-97-98.

DISTANCE BY WAGON ROAD FROM BRADFORD TO SURROUNDING TOWNS.

	Miles.		Miles.
Aiken	9½	Lewis Run	6
Battle City	1½	Limestone	6
Big Shanty	7½	Marshburg	12
Carrollton	12	Mt. Alton	18
Chipmunk	11	Newton's	18½
Clark's Corners	2	Nusbaum's	6
Coleville	9	Olean	18
Corydon	18	Ormsby	16½
Custer City	3½	Red Rock	6
Dallas	5½	Rew City	9
Davis City	8	Riverside	9
DeGolier	3	Rixford	9
Derrick City	4½	Rock City	10
Duke Centre	10½	Sawyer	3½
Eldred	18	Simpson	13½
Gillmor	5	Smethport	18
Klondike, in Watson-		State Line	3½
ville district	16	Summit City	7
Knapps Creek	8	Toad Hollow	2½
Lafayette	11		

RAILROAD INFORMATION.

DISTANCE, FARE AND ROUTE TO PRINCIPAL CITIES FROM BRADFORD, VIA B. R. & P. R. R.

Albany, N. Y.—352 miles, fare $6.49, via Rochester and N. Y. C. & H. R. R. R

Baltimore, Md.—360 miles, fare $10.00, via Johnsonburg and Penn'a Ry.

Boston, Mass.—535 miles, fare $10.99 via Rochester, N. Y. C. & H. R. R. R. and B. & A. R. R. Leave Bradford 2:10 p. m., arrive Boston 10:45 a. m. Also via Rochester, West Shore R. R. to Rotterdam and Hoosac Tunnel Route to Boston. Arrive 10:20 a. m.

Chicago, Ill.—600 miles, fare, 1st class, $12:52; 2nd class, $10:02, via Buffalo and Wabash R. R. Leave Bradford 4:35 p. m., arrive Chicago 9:00 a. m. Free reclining chair cars, Buffalo to Chicago, on 1st or 2nd class tickets.

Cleveland, Ohio.—260 miles, fare $5.52, via Buffalo and N. Y. C. & St. L. R. R.

Detroit, Mich.—328 miles, fare, 1st class, $9.30; 2nd class, $7:30 via Buffalo and Michigan Central R. R., or Wabash R. R., or Grand Trunk R. R.

Hamilton, Ontario.—145 miles, fare $4.25, via Buffalo and N. Y. C. & H. R. R. R. to Suspension Bridge and Grand Trunk R. R.

Harrisburg, Pa.—276 miles, fare $7.81, via Johnsonburg and Penn'a R. R.

35

Lock Haven, Pa.—185 miles, fare $4.27, via Johnsonburg and Penn'a R. R.

Montreal, P. Q. -517 miles, fare $13.55. via Buffalo and N. Y. C. & H. R. R. R. to Suspension Bridge and Grand Trunk R. R.

New York City. 419 miles, fare $8 34, via Rochester and N. Y. C. & H. R. R. R. (Empire State Express.) Leave Bradford 8:10 a. m., arrive 10:00 p. m.

Niagara Falls.—99 miles, fare $2.85, via Buffalo and N. Y. C. & H. R. R. R.

Philadelphia.—382 miles, fare $9.25, via Johnsonburg and Penn'a R. R.

Pittsburg.—211 miles, fare $6 00 via Falls Creek and Allegheny Valley R. R. Also 347 miles. fare $6.00, via Buffalo and W. N. Y. & P. R. R. to Oil City and Allegheny Valley R. R.

Quebec, P. Q.—690 miles, fare $18.05, via Buffalo, N. Y. C. & H. R. R. R. to Suspension Bridge and Grand Trunk R. R.

Syracuse, N. Y.—204 miles, fare $5.19, via Rochester and N. Y. C & H. R. R. R.

St. Louis, Mo.—814 miles, fare, 1st class $18.00: 2nd class $15.02, via Buffalo and Wabash R. R. Free reclining chair cars from Buffalo, 1st or 2nd class tickets. Also 808 miles, fare 1st class, $19.25; 2nd class $16.00, via Buffalo, L. S. & M. S. R. R. to Cleveland and C. C. C. & St. L.

Troy, N. Y.—352 miles, fare $6.49, via Rochester and N. Y, C. & H. R. R. R.

Toledo, Ohio.—376 miles, fare, 1st class, $8.77; 2nd class, $7.07; via Buffalo and L. S. & M. S. R. R.

Toronto Ontario.—184 miles, fare $5.45, via Buffalo, N. Y. C. & H. R. R. R. to Suspension Bridge and· Grand Trunk R. R.

Utica, N. Y.—257 miles, fare $5.94, via Rochester and N. Y. C. & H. R. R. R.

Washington, D. C.—403 miles, fare $10.75, via Johnsonburg and Penn'a R. R.

Williamsport, Pa.—183 miles, fare $5.01, via Johnsonburg and Penn'a R. R.

DISTANCE, FARE AND ROUTE TO PRINCIPAL CITIES FROM BRADFORD, VIA ERIE RAILROAD.

Albany, N. Y.—348 miles. Fare $6.49, via Binghamton, and D. & H. C. R. R. Leaves Bradford 7:15 a. m. and 4:40 p. m., arrives Albany 6:15 p. m. and 6:35 a. m.

Baltimore, Md.—402 miles. Fare $10.00, via Elmira, and Pennsylvania Railroad and Waverly and Lehigh Valley.

Boston, Mass.—539 miles. Fare $10.99, via Binghamton. D. & H. C. and Fitchburg or Boston and Albany. Leaves Bradford 7:10 a. m., 4:40 p. m., arrives Boston 7 a. m. and 3 p. m.

Detroit, Mich.—402 miles. Fare, 1st class, $9.30; 2nd class. $7.30, via Cleveland and L. S. & M. S. Leaves Bradford 6:10 a. m., arrives Detroit 6:20 p. m.

Hamilton, Ontario.—146 miles. Fare $4.25, via Suspension Bridge and Grand Trunk R. R.

Harrisburg, Pa,—317 miles. Fare $7.53, via Elmira and Pennsylvania Railroad.

Lock Haven, Pa.—224 miles. Fare $5.22, via Elmira and Pennsylvania Railroad.

Montreal, P. Q.—556 miles. Fare $12.74, via Binghamton and Rouse's Point railway, and Grand Trunk; also $13.55, via Suspension Bridge and Grand Trunk railway.

Philadelphia, Pa.—423 miles. Fare $9.25, via Elmira and Pennsylvania Railroad, or Waverly and Lehigh Valley and Philadelphia and Reading.

Quebec, P. Q.—690 miles. Fare $18.05, via Suspension Bridge and Grand Trunk.

Syracuse, N. Y.—251 miles. Fare $5.19, via Elmira and Lehigh Valley railroad.

St. Louis, Mo.—814 miles. Fare, 1st class, $18.27; 2nd class, $15.02, via Huntington or Cincinnati.

Troy, N. Y.—348 miles. Fare $6.49, via Binghamton and D. & H. R. R.

Toledo, O.—354 miles. Fare, 1st class, $7.97; 2nd class, $7.07, via Creston and Mansfield; via Cleveland, 1st class, $8.77; 2d class, $7.07, Leaves Bradford 6:10 a. m., arrives Toledo 4 p. m.

Toronto, Ontario.—184 miles. Fare, $5.45 via Suspension Bridge and Grand Trunk.

Utica, N. Y.—284 miles. Fare $6.25, via Binghamton and D., L. & W. railroad.

Washington, D. C.—445 miles. Fare $10.75, via Elmira or Waverly, Penn'a railroad, or L. V. and P. & R.

Williamsport, Pa—224 miles. Fare $4.71, via Elmira and Pennsylvania railroad.

DISTANCE, FARE AND ROUTE TO PRINCIPAL CITIES FROM BRADFORD, VIA W. N. Y. & P. R. R.

Baltimore, Md.—348 miles. Fare $10, via Pennsylvania railroad. Leaves 4 p. m., arrives Baltimore 6:20 a. m.

Brantford, Ont.—Distance 176 miles. Fare $4.85, via Toronto, Hamilton and Buffalo railway. Leaves 9:35 a. m., arrives Brantford 6:35 p. m.

Butler, Pa.—192 miles. Fare $5.45, via P. & W. R. R. Leaves 8:25 a. m. and 4 p. m,, arrives Butler 4:20 p. m., and 7:05 a. m.

Foxburg, Pa.—162 miles. Fare $4.40, via A. V. R. R. Leaves 8:25 a. m. and 4 p. m., arrives Foxburg 3:34 p. m. and 4:31 a. m.

Franklin, Pa.—123 miles. Fare $3.42, via **A. V. R. R.** Leaves 8:25 a. m. and 4 p. m., arrives Franklin 2:25 p. m. and 3:15 a. m.

Hamilton, Ont.—150 miles. Fare $4.25, via Toronto, Hamilton and Buffalo railway. Leaves 9:35 a. m., arrives Hamilton 4 p. m.

Harrisburg, Pa.—263 miles. Fare $7.81, via Pennsylvania railroad. Leaves 9:35 a. m. and 4 p. m., arrives Harrisburg 10:10 p. m. and 3:22 a. m.

Parker, Pa.—165 miles. Fare $4 50, via **A. V. R. R.** Leaves 8:25 a. m. and 4:00 p. m., arrives Parker 3:40 p. m. and 4:38 a. m.

Philadelphia, Pa.—368 miles. Fare $9.25, via Pennsylvania. railroad. Leaves 4 p. m , arrives Phila. 6:50 a. m.

Pittsburg, Pa.—240 miles. Fare $6, via **A. V. R R.** Leaves 8:25 a. m. and 4 p. m., arrives Pittsburg 6:30 p. m. and 7:20 a. m,

Titusville, Pa. - 95 miles. Fare $2.82, via D., **A. V. & P. R. R.** Leaves 8:25 a. m. and 4 p. m., arrives Titusville 12:15 and 9:15 p. m.

Toronto, Ont.—190 miles. Fare $5.45, via Buffalo and Canadian Pacific railway. Leave 9:35 a. m., arrives Toronto 5 p. m.

Washington, D. C.—391 miles. Fare $10 75, via Pennsylvania railroad. Leaves 4 p. m., arrives Washington 7:40 a. m.

Wheeling, W. Va.—308 miles. Fare $8, via P., C., C. & St. L. R'y. Leaves 8:25 a. m. and 4 p. m., arrives Wheeling 8:05 p. m. and 8:30 a. m.

Williamsport, Pa.—170 miles. Fare $5.01, via Pennsylvania railroad. Leaves 9:35 a. m, and 4 p. m., arrives Williamsport 6:45 p. m. and 12:05 midnight.

DISTANCE AND FARE TO POINTS ON B., B. & K. R. R.

From Bradford to

	Miles.	Fare.
Tarport Hill	3 88	$ 15
Chapin	5.14	20
Hazelwood	5.98	25
Forest	6.45	25
Taylor	7.65	30
Kinzua Junction	9.90	40
Allen's	11.01	45
Aiken	11.54	45
Davis	13.22	50
Van Vleck's	14.31	55
Simpson	15.31	60
Cyclone	16.04	64
McKean's	17.38	64
Ormsby Junction	18.68	64
Crystal Hill	21.90	75
Smethport	25.74	95
Nearing's	22.33	64
Kinzua Bridge	24.31	64
McAmbley's	25.40	64

Mt. Jewett	28.64	64
Lafayette	31.93	80
Griffith's	33.93	85
Kanesholm	35.93	95
Cartwright's	36.00	95
Greendale	38.13	1 00
Kane Junction	40.73	1 15
Kane	41.43	1 15

Distance and Fare to Points on Pittsburg and Western Railroad, via B., B. & K. R. R., Changing at Kane.

From Bradford to

	Miles.	Fare.
Kane	41	$1 15
Russell City	54	1 70
Sheffield Junction	59.50	1 90
McCray's	71	2 40
Marienville	73	2 45
Vowinkle	81	2 75
Tylersburg	87	3 00
Clarion	105	3 75
Foxburg	124	4 40
Parker	126	4 50
Petrolia	135	4 85
Butler	154	5 50
Callery Junction	168	6 00
Allegheny	194	6 00

Distance and Fare to Points on Pennsylvania Railroad, via B., B. & K. R. R., Changing at Kane.

From Bradford to

	Miles.	Fare.
Kane	41	$ 1 15
Johnsonburg	57	1 61
Ridgway	65	1 85
St. Mary's	76	2 16
Emporium	96	2 15
Renova	142	3 43
Lock Haven	170	4 27
Jersey Shore	183	4 66
Williamsport	195	5 01
Sunbury	235	6 20
Harrisburg	288	7 81
Lancaster	324	8 89
Philadelphia	393	9 25
York	315	8 66
Baltimore, Md	372	10 00
Washington, D. C	416	10 75

DISTANCE AND FARE TO POINTS ON B., R. & P. R. R.

Buffalo Division. From Bradford to

	Miles.	Fare.
East Bradford	1	$ 05
State Line	3	10
Limestone	5	16

	Miles.	Fare.
Riverside Park.,	9	30
Carrollton	11	34
Killbuck	15	45
Salamanca	17	52
S. & B Junction	16	48
Great Valley	20	61
Ellicottville	25	75
Ashford	29	89
West Valley	36	1 08
Riceville	38	1 15
Hoyts	40	1 20
Springville	45	1 36
East Concord	49	1 46
Glenwood	53	1 60
Golden	55	1 67
West Falls	60	1 82
Jewettville	61	1 85
Orchard Park	66	1 98
Windom	69	2 08
West Seneca	72	2 16
Buffalo Creek	75	2 24
Buffalo	77	2 30

Rochester Division. From Braddford to

	Miles.	Fare.
Ashford	29	$ 89
Devereux	32	96
Summit	35	1 04
Machias	40	1 20
Elton	41	1 30
Farmersville	48	1 42
Freedom	52	1 55
Eagle	57	1 71
Bliss	60	1 80
Pike	66	1 96
Gainesville	69	2 07
Silver Springs	75	2 23
Silver Lake Junction	74	2 20
Rock Glen	75	2 25
Warsaw	80	2 38
Saltvale	83	2 47
Wyoming	85	2 55
Pearl Creek	88	2 63
Pavilion	91	2 70
Pavilion Centre	93	2 77
D., L. & W. Junction	94	2 81
Lehigh	95	2 85
LeRoy	99	2 94
Lime Rock	103	3 05
P. & L. Junction	105	3 15
State Fish Pond Cr's	106	.....
Mumford	107	3 17
Wheatland	108	3 22
Garbuttsville	110	3 57
Scottsville	112	3 34
Brookdale	116	3 47
Maplewood	119	3 53
Lincoln Park	122	3 64
Rochester	124	3 70

Pittsburg Division. From Bradford to

	Miles.	Fare.
DeGolia	3	$ 10
Custer City	4	10
Howard	5	15
Emery	6	18
Dent	10	25
Bingham	13	35
Newton	16	40
Boyer	21	50
McAmbly's	22	55
Mt. Jewett	25	64
Freeman	28	71
Gallagher's	30	77
Hutchins	31	81
Midmont	35	92
Rasselas	36	97
Streight's	39	1 05
Ketner	42	1 12
Johnsonburg	46	1 26
Whistletown	51	1 40
Ridgway	55	1 50
Mill Creek	58	1 65
Carman	62	1 75
Empire	65	1 80
Ellmont	67	1 85
Carrier	69	1 95
Brockwayville	73	2 05
Lane's Mills	75	2 13
Beech Tree Junction	76	2 15
Grove Summit	79	2 20
Falls Creek	85	2 40
DuBois	87	2 45
DuBois Junction	90	2 55
Stanley	93	2 65
Helvetia	94	2 70
Sykes	95	2 70
Cramer	97	2 80
Big Run	102	2 90
Bell's Mills	105	3 00
Punxsutawney	109	3 10
Lindsey	110	3 10
Walston	111	3 15

Clearfield and Mahoning Division. From Bradford to

	Miles.	Fare.
DuBois	87	2 45
DuBois Junction	90	2 55
Salem	91	2 60
Luthersburg	93	2 65
Rockton	96	2 75
Anderson Viaduct	97	2 80
Blooms	98	2 90
Bridgeport	106	3 05
Curwensville	108	3 10
Centre	111	3 25
Clearfield—Market street	114	3 25
" Beech Creek railroad depot	116	3 25

DISTANCE AND FARE TO POINTS ON ERIE RAILROAD.

Bradford Division—Going North. From Bradford to

	Miles.	Fare.
East Bradford	1.2	$ 05
Limestone	5.1	16
Riverside Park	8.9	30
Carrollton	11.2	34

Bradford Division—Going South. From Bradford to

	Miles.	Fare.
DeGolia	3.0	09
Custer City	3.5	10
Howard Junction	4.9	15
Lewis Run	5.8	18
Big Shanty	7.7	23
Crawford Junction	12.1	37
Alton	13.8	44
Buttsville	15.3	47
Riderville	13.7	41
Kinzua Viaduct	16.2	49
Fraley's	17.7	64
Mt. Jewett	21.1	64
Freeman	23.5	71
Hutchins	26.9	81
Midmont	30.5	92
Rasselas	32.1	97
Ketner	37.3	1 12
Clarion Junction	41.1	1 24
Johnsonburg	42.0	1 26

Main Line Erie—Going East. From Bradford to

	Miles.	Fare.
Carrollton	11	34
Olean	24	64
Cuba	36	1 09
Friendship	45	1 34
Wellsville	60	1 84
Hornellsville	87	2 64
Addison	117	3 44
Corning	128	3 49
Elmira	145	3 49
Waverly	163	4 04
Owego	182	4 59
Union	196	4 99
Binghamton	204	5 19
Susquehanna	227	5 89
Deposit	242	6 34
Hancock	255	6 74
Callicoon	283	7 49
Lackawaxen	308	8 19
Shohola	312	8 19
Port Jervis	331	8 19
New York City	419	8 34

Main Line Erie—Going West. From Bradford to

	Miles.	Fare.
Carrollton	11	34
Salamanca	17	52
Jamestown	51	1 52

Lakewood	56	1 67
Corry	77	2 32
Union City...	89	2 67
Cambridge Springs................................	105	3 17
Saegertown........................	113	3 42
Meadville.......	119	3 42
Youngstown....................................	175	5 27
Warren..	190	5 37
Cleveland...	242	5 52
Akron	230	6 57
Creston..	254	7 07
Mansfield...	296	7 77
Marion Junction................................	333	8 52
Dayton	416	11 07
Cincinnati..........	575	11 52
Lima...	385	9 82
Ohio City..	412	9 52
Huntington..	460	11 82
Chicago	602	12 52

DISTANCE AND FARE TO POINTS ON W., N. Y. & P. R. R.

Buffalo Division—Going North.   From Bradford to

	Miles.	Fare.
East Bradford.......................................	1	$ 05
Limestone..	5	16
Riverside Junction..............................	10	30
South Vandalia...................................	12	38
Allegany...	18	55
Olean...	21	64
Hinsdale...	23	84
Ischua........	34	1 02
Franklinville........	42	1 27
Machias Junction..................................	47	1 42
Delevan...	53	1 60
Arcade...	56	1 69
Chaffee......	59	1 78
Protection..	61	1 84
Holland..	65	1 96
South Wales.......................................	70	2 16
East Aurora..	74	2 26
Jamison Road......................................	77	2 30
Elma...	79	2 30
Springbrook......................................	81	2 30
Ebenezer..	85	2 30
South Buffalo......................................	87	2 30
D., L. & W. Crossing.............................	89	2 30
Buffalo..	91	2 30

Buffalo Division—Going South.   From Bradford to

	Miles.	Fare.
Olean	21	64
Weston's...	24	76
Portville...	27	82
Bullis' Mills..	30	91
Eldred...	35	1 06
Larrabee's..	38	1 15
Smethport..	44	1 42

Turtle Point	42	1 27
Port Allegany	47	1 42
Liberty	55	1 65
Keating Summit	58	1 74
Gardeau	63	1 90
Shippen	65	1 96
Emporium	72	2 15

River Division. From Bradford to

	Miles.	Fare.
Riverside Junction	10	30
South Carrollton	12	35
Salamanca	17	52
Red House	23	70
Quaker Bridge	29	87
Wolf Run	31	93
Onoville	34	1 02
Corydon	37	1 11
Sugar Run	43	1 31
Kinzua	45	1 37
Hemlock	52	1 56
Glade	55	1 67
Struthers	57	1 71
Warren	59	1 75
Irvineton	64	1 92
Thompson's	71	2 12
Tidioute	79	2 37
Trunkeyville	84	2 53
Hickory	87	2 62
Tionesta	93	2 81
Hunter	96	2 90
President	101	3 03
Eagle Rock	102	3 06
Oleopolis	105	3 24
Rockwood	110	3 32
Siverly	113	3 40
Oil City	114	3 42

Twenty-four passenger trains leave Bradford daily, except Sunday.

Twenty passenger trains arrive in Bradford daily, except Sunday.

'The Bradford Division of the Erie Railroad was completed in 1865. It is the pioneer road of the city.

It is estimated that the combined monthly pay rolls of the different railroads in Bradford is over $50,000.

In 1863 an ordinary hand-car was used to convey passengers, baggage and freight from Bradford to Carrollton and back. This was afterward improved on in the shape of a home-made train. The necessary car wheels were secured and an ordinary combination boiler and engine rigged up on a flat car, which by an ingenious arrangement of shafts, pulleys and belts, furnished the motive power.

DISTANCE AND FARE FROM BRADFORD TO ONE IMPORTANT CITY IN ANY STATE IN THE UNION.—Via B. R. & P. R. R.

State.	City.	Distance. Miles.	Railroad Fare. First Class.	Second Class.
Arizona	Phœnix	2574	$ 72 67	$ 62 44
Arkansas	Little Rock	1153	26 04	24 12
Alabama	Montgomery	1075	24 27	22 02
Alaska Ter				
California	San Francisco	2957	75 02	62 52
Colorado	Denver	1679	42 02	38 52
Connecticut	Hartford	481	9 33	
Delaware	Wilmington	408	10 00	
Dist. Columbia	Washington	403	10 75	
Florida	Jacksonville	889	30 02	28 02
Georgia	Atlanta	1051	20 77	18 52
Idaho	Boise City	2446	70 02	57 52
Illinois	Chicago	600	12 52	10 02
Indiana	Indianapolis	543	12 52	11 22
Iowa	DesMoines	963	21 67	20 17
Indian Ter				
Kansas	Topeka	1106	26 52	23 02
Kentucky	Frankfort	596	14 22	
Louisiana	New Orleans	1305	29 77	26 27
Maine	Bangor	786	16 99	
Massachusetts	Boston	535	10 99	
Maryland	Baltimore	360	1(00	
Missouri	Kansas City	1039	25 02	21 52
Minnesota	St. Paul	1008	24 02	21 52
Montana	Helena	2185	59 02	
Michigan	Lansing	416	10 21	8 66
Mississippi	Jackson	1204	28 77	25 27
Nebraska	Omaha	1093	25 27	22 77
Nevada	Carson City	2744		
New Hampshire	Concord	640	12 59	
New Jersey	Trenton	477	8 34	
New Mexico	Santa Fe	1908	53 57	42 87
New York	New York City	419	8 34	
North Carolina	Raleigh	700	20 40	
North Dakota	Bismarck	1452	39 12	31 52
Ohio	Cincinnati	475	11 52	
Oklahoma Ter	Oklahoma City	1439	35 62	32 02
Oregon	Portland	2914	74 02	61 52
Pennsylvania	Philadelphia	382	9 25	
Rhode Island	Providence	554	11 15	
South Carolina	Columbia	889	26 05	
South Dakota	Sioux Falls	1117	27 52	25 02
Tennessee	Nashville	771	20 52	19 02
Texas	Galveston	1677	39 62	31 52
Utah	Salt Lake City	2161	54 02	51 52
Vermont	Montpelier	588	11 44	
Virginia	Richmond	519	14 25	
Washington	Seattle	2940	74 02	61 52
West Virginia	Wheeling	282	8 00	
Wisconsin	Milwaukee	685	15 07	12 57
Wyoming	Cheyenne	1609	41 07	38 67

RAILROAD TIME TABLES.

BRADFORD, BORDELL AND KINZUA RAILROAD.

Trains Leave Erie Depot:

7:30 A. M. Mail and express daily, except Sunday, for Kinzua Junction, Aiken, Davis, Simpson, Ormsby Junction, Smethport, Mt Jewett and Kane. Connecting with Pittsburg and Western, leaving Kane, 10:30 a. m. for Russell City, Sheffield Junction, Clarion, Foxburg, Butler, Pittsburg; arriving at Pittsburg, 7:20 p. m. Also connects with Pennsylvania Railroad, leaving Kane at 11:10 a. m. for Wilcox, Johnsonburg, Ridgway, St. Mary's, Emporium, Renova, Lock Haven, Williamsport, Sunbury, and Harrisburg; arriving at Harrisburg at 10:10 p. m.

1:45 P. M. Express daily, except Sunday, for Smethport, Mt. Jewett, Kane and intermediate points, arriving at Kane at 4:00 p. m.

4:30 P. M. Mail and express daily for Smethport, Mt. Jewett, Kane and intermediate points. Connecting with Pennsylvania Railroad, leaving Kane at 7:10 p m. for Wilcox, Johnsonburg, Ridgway, St. Mary's, Emporium, Renova, Lock Haven, Williamsport, Sunbury, Harrisburg, Philadelphia, arriving at Philadelphia at 6:52 a. m. Also connects at Harrisburg for Baltimore and Washington, arriving at Washington at 7:40 a. m., Baltimore 6:20 a. m.

Trains Arrive at Bradford, Erie depot, from Kane and Smethport and intermediate points at 10:00 a. m. daily and 12:25 p. m.; and at 7:10 p. m. daily, except Sunday, from Kane, Smethport, Pittsburg, Butler, Foxburg, Clarion and intermediate stations.

W. L. WELLS, Ticket Agent,

JOHN C. McKENNA,   Erie Railway Depot,

Gen. Passenger Agent,   Bradford, Pa.

Bradford, Pa.

BUFFALO, ROCHESTER AND PITTSBURG RAILWAY.

Trains Depart:

6:50 A. M. Accommodation; daily, except Sunday, for Custer City, Lewis Run, Big Shanty, Riterville, Kinzua Bridge, Mt. Jewett, Johnsonburg, Ridgway, Brockwayville, Falls Creek, DuBois, Curwensville, Clearfield, Punxsutawney.

8:10 A. M. Buffalo and Rochester Express. Daily, except Sunday, for for Salamanca, Ellicottville, Springville, Buffalo, Warsaw, LeRoy and Rochester.

12:30 P.M. Mail. Daily, except Sunday, for Custer City, Emery's, Dent, Bingham's, Mt. Jewett, Johnsonburg, Ridgway, Brockwayville, Beechtree, Falls Creek, DuBois, Big Run, Punxsutawney, Clearfield and Walston.

2:10 P. M. Mail. Daily, except Sunday, for Limestone, Carrollton, Salamanca. Ellicottville, Warsaw, LeRoy, Rochester, New York and Boston.

4:35 P. M. Chicago Express Daily, for Salamanca, Springville, Buffalo, Pittsburg and Chicago.

3:00 P. M. Buffalo Express. Sunday only, for Salamanca, Springville, Buffalo, Pittsburg, Toledo and Chicago.

Trains Arrive:

11:15 a. m.—Mail from Buffalo; daily, except Sunday.

11:55 a. m.—Rochester mail; daily, except Sunday.

11:55 a. m.—Sunday Express, from Buffalo.

1:45 p. m.—Mail, from DuBois and Punxsutawney; daily, except Sunday.

4:30 p. m.—Accommodation, from Punxsutawney and Pittsburg; daily, except Sunday.

8:40 p. m.—Express, from Buffalo and Rochester, daily, except Sunday.

E. C. LAPEY,	L. B. MCINTYRE,
Gen. Pass. Agent,	Agent, B., R. & P. Depot,
Rochester, N. Y.	Bradford, Pa.

Trains Depart:

6:10 A. M. Daily for Corry, Erie, Titusville, Meadville, Cleveland, Pittsburg and points west.

6:55 A. M. Daily. The Vestibuled Limited, East for Hornellsville, Elmira, Binghamton, New York, Philadelphia, Albany, Boston, and all points East and South. Pullman Palace and Dining cars. Pullman Sleeper to Boston.

7:10 A. M. Daily. Accommodation for Hornells and all intermediate stations. Connecting for Corning, Elmira, Binghamton and New York.

10:25 A. M. Daily. For Corry, Titusville, Meadville, Franklin, Oil City. Pittsburg, Cleveland, Chicago, Cincinnati and all points West. Connects for Dunkirk and intermediate stations. Pullman Sleepers to Chicago and Cincinnati.

10:25 A. M. Daily. For New York and intermediate stations.

2:15 P. M. Daily. Accommodation for Hornellsville and intermediate stations.

3 15 P. M. Daily, except Sunday. For Jamestown, Corry, Meadville, Titusville, Oil City. Also for Dayton, Dunkirk and Buffalo.

5:35 P. M. Daily. For New York, Philadelphia, Albany, Troy, Boston, Baltimore, Washington and all points East and South. Pullman cars to New York and Albany.

8:00 P. M. Daily. For Salamanca. Also East for Olean, Hornellsville, Elmira, Binghamton, New York. Pullman cars to New York.

12:30 P. M. Way train, daily, except Sunday, for Alton and all intermediate stations.

Trains Arrive from the East at *7:20 a. m. From the West, *9:25 a. m. From East and West, †11:47 a. m. From West, 12:10 p. m. From East and West, *4:12 p. m. From West, *6:40 p. m. From East and West, *9:10 p. m. From the South, †3:55 p. m.

* Daily; † Except sunday.

D I. ROBERTS,   W. L. WELLS,
   General Passenger Agent,   Agent at Bradford.
       New York City.   H. T. JAEGER,
           General Agent Passenger Department.
               Buffalo, N. Y.

ALL STOVES.

These are facts that mean much.

We carry 50 styles of heaters in stock here from $3.00 up.

That means that you can get what you want here.

We sell 500 Stoves per year.

That means that we can buy lowest, and that people know that we sell lowest.

The most popular gas heater ever sold in Bradford is the Radiant Home No. 20---$14.

We are exclusive agents.

The best range on any market--- best in twenty different ways---is the Reliable.

No one else sells it.

The only "pure air" heaters are sold here.

The only mantel heaters, too.

People know that we know what good stoves are. We will tell you all about them when you come here.

EMERY & WEAVER,
L. EMERY, JR. & CO.,
BRADFORD, PA.

Mead.
and points

East
Binghamton,
bany, Bos-
and South.
cars. Pull-

for Hornells-
les. Connect-
Binghamton

Meadville,
Cleveland,
nts West.
Intermediate
to Chicago

and intermediate

for Hornells-
us.

r Jamestown,
Oil City.
and Buffalo.

Philadelphia,
more, Wash-
and South.
and Albany.

Also East for
Bingham-
rs to New

Sunday, for
stations.

From the West.
a. m. From
4:12 p. m.
West, 9:10

at Bradford.

rtment.

It's Hard to Believe

That you can get a book which combines a History, a Railroad Guide, a Complete Business Directory, and in fact an Encyclopædia of your own city, and in a form which you can carry in your pocket. . . . . . .

But It's a Fact

That THE BOOK OF BRADFORD is just such a work, as a glance into this volume will prove. From cover to cover it is full of information. If you want to embark on a journey and wish to know the route to take, the railroad to travel over, the time your train leaves, the connections you'll have to make, and the distance and railroad fare you can find it here. If you want to know who is engaged in any certain line of business you can refer to the Business Directory. If you are looking up some important event in the city's history you will find it under "Historical Notes." If you want to know anything about Bradford . . . . . , .

It's In the Book,

If you have a friend or a relative whom you would like to have know something about your city or your busines send him a copy. If you have a few good customers in the country what better way of showing your appreciation of their trade than by presenting them with a copy of THE BOOK OF BRADFORD. It would be a handy book for them.

If you wish one or more extra copies of the book address

F. M. McDonnell, ⁄ Publisher, ⁄ Bradford.

WESTERN NEW YORK AND PENNSYLVANIA RAILROAD,

Trains Depart:

8:25 A. M. Pittsburg Express. Daily, except Sunday, for Salamanca, Warren, Titusville, Oil City, Franklin, Emlenton, Foxburg, Kittanning, New Castle and Pittsburg. Arrive Pittsburg 6:30 p. m.

9:35 A. M. Buffalo Express. Daily, except Sunday, for Olean, Buffalo, Smethport, Coudersport, Emporium, Lock Haven, Williamsport and Harrisburg. Arrive Harrisburg 10:10 p. m.

3:00 P. M. Buffalo and Rochester Express. Daily, except Sunday, for Olean, Buffalo and Rochester. Arrive Buffalo, 6:30 p. m.; Rochester, 8:00 p. m.

4:00 P. M. Southern Express. Daily, except Sunday, for Salamanca, Warren, Titusville, Oil City, Olean, Bolivar, Smethport, Coudersport, Austin, Emporium Williamsport, Philadelphia, Baltimore and Washington. Arrive Philadelphia, 6:52 a. m.; Baltimore, 6;20 a. m.: Washington, 7:40 a. m.

7:20 P. M. Olean Accommodation. Daily, except Sunday, arriving at Olean at 8:05 p. m.

Trains Arrive from Olean at 6:00, 9:08 a. m., 12:21, 6:55 p.m. From Buffalo at 12:21 and 6:55 p. m. From Oil City 12:21 and 8:01 p. m.

Sunday Trains—Leave Bradford 9:30 a. m , 3:10 p. m. Arrive 12:35 and 5:55 p. m.

For tickets and full information call on J. A. McKARNES, Agent, Bradford, Pa.

J. A. FELLOWS, Gen. Pass. and Ticket Agent.
R. BELL, General Superintendent,
Buffalo, N. Y.

___

OLEAN, ROCK CITY AND BRADFORD STREET RAILROAD.

Cars Leave Bradford.---First car at 6:30 a. m. and every two hours thereafter daily, until 8:30 p. m. First car leaves Sunday at 8:30 a. m.

Cars Arrive at Bradford.---First car at 8:30 a. m. and every two hours thereafter until 10:30 p. m. daily. First car arrives Sunday at 10:30 a. m.

ISAAC B. WHITE, Superintendent.

RAILWAY DEPOTS.

Allegheny & Kinzua Railway.—M. D. Murray, superintendent; J. B. Murray, freight agent. Passenger and freight depots cor. Washington and A. & K. R. R. Tel. 174.

Sugar Run Railway.—C. V. Merrick, superintendent; M. D. Murray, assistant superintendent. Passenger and freight depots cor. Washington aud A. & K. R. R. Tel. 174.

Bradford, Bordell and Kinzua Railway.—J. C. McKenna, general manager, freight and passenger agent. Passenger depot cor. Main and Railroad ave. (Erie.) Freight depot foot Chestnut. Tel. 208. ·

Erie Railroad.—W. L. Wells, passenger agent; John J. Crowley, ticket agent; B. J. Cato, freight agent. Passenger depot cor. Main and Railroad ave. Tel. 162-B. Freight depot on Webster, near Elm. Tel. 162.

Western New York and Pennsylvania Railroad.—John McKarnes, Passenger and freight agent. Passenger and freight depots Main, cor. Railroad. Tel. 87.

Buffalo, Rochester and Pittsburg Railway.— L. B. McIntyre, passenger and freight agent; P. N. McCarthy, cashier; C. C. Stratton, ticket clerk. Passenger and freight depots Main, cor. railroad. Tel. 243.

Buffalo, Rochester and Pittsburg Railway.—East End depot. S. D. Sexsmith, agent. Cor. Kendall ave. and railroad.

Erie Railroad.—East End depot. J. Collins, agent. Cor. Kendall ave. and railroad.

Olean, Rock City and Bradford Railway Company.—Office and depot at 1 Main, cor. Mechanic. Tel. 270.

Bradford Electric Street Railway Company.—Office and depot at 1 Main, cor. Mechanic. Tel. 270.

HINTS TO TRAVELERS.

Half fare is charged for children between the ages of 5 and 12. Children under 5 are carried free.

Baggage to the amount of 150 pounds is allowed on each full ticket and 75 pounds on each half ticket.

Always have your name marked plainly on your trunk and make memorandum of check numbers, for if you should lose your check you will have to prove your property.

If you wish to stop over at any point and your ticket allows it, you must ask the conductor for a stop-over check; otherwise your ticket will be no good on continuing your journey.

BUSINESS DIRECTORY.

ADVERTISING DISTRIBUTOR.

M. K. Walker, Distributor of all kinds of advertising matter, 130 Mechanic.

ARCHITECTS.

E. N. Unruh, 8 Phœnix block, over 1 Main.

E. F. Brickell, 13 Phœnix block, over 1 Main.

Peter McManus, Jr., 112 Washington Extension.

ART AND FANCY WORK.

Misses Spence & Ellis (Minnie E. Spence, Bella Ellis), Art and fancy goods and fancy work materials. Artistic stamping and embroidery done. 57 Main.

ARTISTS.

Mrs. L. E. Howard, China decorator and teacher in oils and drawing. Studio 23 Jefferson.

Miss Martha F. Kern, China decorator and teacher. Studio 21 Chautauqua place.

Miss Bess Goe, Studio 218 So. Mechanic.

ATTORNEYS-AT-LAW.

Brown & Schoonmaker (W. W. Brown, F. P. Schoonmaker), Attorneys-at-law and notaries public. Offices 1-2, Phœnix block, 1 Main.

J. M. McClure, Attorney-at-law. Offices 3-4 Phœnix block, 1 Main.

D. H. Jack, Attorney-at-law and notary public. Office over 11 Main. Tel. 203.

M. H. Byles, Attorney-at-law and notary public. Office over 9 Main. Tel. 178.

Mullin & Mullin (Eugene, John P., Eugene W. and Timothy F.), Attorneys-at-Law and notary public. Offices over Commercial Bank, 15 Main. Tel. 269.

C. E. Judd, Attorney-at law and notary public. Office over 19 Main.

C. J. Curtis, Attorney-at-law, real estate, collections, loans, etc. Office over 28 Main.

F. W. Hastings, Attorney-at-law and notary public. Office, room 5, over 32 Main. Entrance on Congress.

F. W. Hastings, Jr., Attorney-at-law, notary public, collector state and county taxes (1897). Office, room 6, over 32 Main. Entrance on Congress.

W. T. Hastings, Attorney-at-law and notary public. Office, room 4, over 32 Main. Entrance on Congress.

J. K. Wilson, Attorney-at-law. Office over 34-36 Main, Dikeman block.

W. J. Milliken, Attorney-at-law. Office, 402 East Main.

Cotter & Shearman (P. R. Cotter, E. H. Shearman), Attorneys-at-law. Office hours 10 to 12 a. m., 1:30 to 4:30 and 7 to 8 p. m. Offices, 1 and 2 Davis block, over 21 Main.

John P. Melvin, Attorney-at-law. Office. 3 Berry & Melvin block, over 18 Main. Tel. 192.

Rufus B. Stone, Attorney-at-law. Office, Pompelon Hall, Public Square. Tel. 249-B.

Lester H. Simons, Attorney-at-law and notary public. Office, Pompelon Hall, Public Square, Tel. 249-B.

W. E. Burdick, Attorney-at-law, notary public. Office, 14 Rosenberg & Michael block, over 48 Main. Tel. 6.

Edwin E. Tait, Attorney-at-law. Office, room 5, Producers' Exchange, Public Square.

Berry & Edgett (G. A. Berry, R L. Edgett), Attorneys-at-law and notary public. Offices, 1-2 Berry & Melvin block, over 18 Main. Tel. 283.

W. B. Chapman, Attorney-at-law. Offices, 6-8 Rosenberg & Michael block, over 46 Main.

James George, Attorney-at-law. Office over 7 Main. Tel. 19.

Moses Sullivan, Attorney-at-law. Loans and collections. Over 29 Main Tel. 268.

Samuel T. Swartz, Attorney-at-law. 124 So. Mechanic, Pompelon Hall. Tel. 160.

J. H. Cunningham, Attorney-at-law. Over 16 Congress.

H. King, Attorney-at-law. Office. 1 Bradburn block, over 95 Main.

W. J. King, Attorney-at-law. Pompelon Hall. Tel. 249-B.

C. D. Longfellow, Attorney-at-law. 161 Kendall ave.

Loyal Ward, Attorney-at-law, real estate and collections. Office, 81 Mechanic.

H. H. North, Attorney-at-law, Office, 1-2 Sheehy block, over 110 Mechanic.

AUCTION AND COMMISSION.

W. A. Hutchinson, Auction and commission house. 97 Main.

BAKERS.

Keystone Bakery, W. D. Russell, propr. 119 Main.

W. J. O'Neill, Baker. Also confectionery, tobacco and cigars. 81 Mechanic.

French Bakery, Myron Carroll, propr. Also confectionery. 64 Corydon.

Mrs. G. N. Storey, Domestic Bakery. 95 Washington.

Vienna Bakery, C. Schneider, propr. Bread, pies and cakes, confectionery and cigars. Lunch room attached. 99 Mechanic, Tel 235.

Mrs. A. E. Fisher, Home-made bakery and creamery, Cigars and confectionery. 57 Mechanic.

Robert Jones, Home bakery. 90 Washington.

Mrs. T. C. Mosher, Home-made Bakery. 13 Bank.

Samuel Blair, Home-made bread, butter, eggs, cheese, etc. 24 Chestnut.

Mrs. M. C. Seeley, Home-made Bread. Wholesale and retail. 45 Kennedy.

J. Wichensky, 105 Washington.

Medberry & London, 163 Main.

BAGGAGE AND PASSENGER TRANSFER LINES.

George M. Riser, Baggage and hack line to and from all trains. Office, St. James Hotel. Tel. 261.

Bradford Transfer Company, Frank Fowler, propr. Baggage, hack and carriage line. Carriages at all hours. 17 Congress. Tel. 236.

BANKS.

Bradford National Bank, Capital $200,000. O. F. Schonblom, president; Thomas H. Kennedy, vice president; Harvey J. Haggerty, cashier; Claude E. Mitchell, assistant cashier. 67 Main. Tel. 298.

Banca Italiana, Caterina & Co., 75 Mechanic.

Commercial National Bank, Capital $100,000. C. H. Lavens, president; Charles Duke, vice president; W. H. Powers, cashier; R. L. Mason, assistant cashier. Cor. Main and Pine. Tel. 296.

First National Bank, Capital $150.000. F. W. Davis, president; C. C. Melvin, vice president; W.W. Bell, cashier; George H. Mills, assistant cashier. Exchange Lyceum building, 31 Main. Tel. 297.

BARBERS.

Kramer & Barnes (J. L. Kramer, W. E. Barnes), 107 Mechanic.

Charles Brown, Shaving parlors and bath, 63 Main.

A. Gillis, 103 Mechanic.

Lisman & Meade, 101 Main.

John Ardizonne, 111 Main.

Raymond Beigel, St. James Hotel Barber.

F. C. Bendeau, 121½ Main, Riddell House block.

John Kramer, 135 Main.

M. W. Albert, 4 Main, Public Square.

Fred Collins, 18 Pine.

E. Sorrentino, 12 Congress.

J. E. Beigel, 3 Kennedy.
C. M. Newman, 4 Webster.

Richard Sheckels, 69 Mechanic.

John W. Collins, 113 Washington.

Little Casino Parlor Shop, Fred G. Zeiss, propr., 4 Barbour, next to United States Hotel.

Thomas Thompson, 106 Washingon.

Mike Leary, 134 Main.

Ardizonne & Pascarella (Joseph Ardizonne, Philip Pascarella), 9 East Main.

H. Martin, 86 Mechanic.

Charles F. Genthner, 3 St. James Place.

John Keelan, 119 Washington.

Don Antico, 110 Washington.

Charles Anderson, 38 Main.

George L. Meyers, 416 East Main.

D. Manguso, 8 High.

Samuel Ames, 115½ Main.

S. Felo, 2 Congress.

S. Marino, 5 Webster.

E. Schoonover, 395 East Main.

BATH HOUSES.

Charles Brown, Tub baths, 63 Main.

Oriental Bath Parlors, A. J. Enty, propr. Turkish, Russian, • ozone, electric, tub and shower, and Hot Springs mineral baths. 67 Corydon. Tel. 14-B.

BILL POSTERS.

Wagner & Reis, 54 Main.

BICYCLE DEALERS AND REPAIRERS.

L. Emery, Jr., & Co., 43-45 Main. Tel. 274.

H. A. Harvey, 113 Main.

M. A. Woodbury, Dealer in bicycles and repairer. Riding school and ice rink in connection. 41-45 Mechanic. Tel. 195.

John Doty, Bicycles. Repairing a specialty. 18 Pine.

J. M. Stevenson, Bicycle repairing, 10 Congress.

The McElwaine Co., Ltd., Bicycle dealers and repairers. Cor. Railroad ave., Newell and Corydon. Tel. 135-B.

R. J. Wagner, Bicycle and general repair shop, 88 Corydon

W. E. Henry, Bicycles, type writers and typewriters' supplies. 88 Corydon.

BILLIARDS AND POOL.

St. James Hotel, Head Main.

Riddell House, Main, cor. Davis.

F. E. Bradley, 38 Main.

Delaney & Mattson (R. C. Delaney, J. H. Mattson), Billiards and pool, tobacco and cigars. 7 Webster.

J. B. Johnson, 181 E. Main.

J. H. Newcomb, 418 East Main.

F. C. Baker, Billiards and pool. 56 Main; upstairs.

J. H. Keefer, Billiards, pool, tobacco and cigars. 135 Main.

BOARDING HOUSES.

Mrs. K. Wittenstein, Over 29 Main.

Mrs. S. M. Crull, Over 50 Main.

Holmes House, Mrs. E. Holmes, propr. 53 Congress. Tel. 241.

The Washburn, Adelaide P. Washburn, propr. 84 Corydon.

BOOKSELLERS AND STATIONERS.

Brennan & Davis (C. M. Brennan, F. G. Davis), Booksellers and stationers. Picture frames, jewelry and bric-a-brac. Blank books and office supplies. Newspapers, magazines and periodicals. Sole agents for Butterick's patterns. 21 Main.

W. L. Field, Bookseller and stationer. All the newspapers, magazines and periodicals. Office supplies. Jewelry and watch repairing. 110 Main.

C. V. Cottrell (Successor to Davis & Cottrell), Books, stationery, office supplies and newspapers. (See druggists.) 95 Main. Tel. 148.

John C. Calhoun & Son, Newsdealers, stationers and booksellers. (See druggists.) 412 East Main. Public Tel.

D. F. Hart, Stationery and office supplies. 434 E. Main. (See druggists.)

BOOT AND SHOE DEALERS.

Lines' Boot and Shoe House (W. H. & S. V. Lines). Ed. G. Bachtel, manager. 50 Main.

George A. Groves, Fine shoes, rubbers, trunks, valises, etc. 51 Main.

Temple Shoe Store, D. Healey, propr. Boots, shoes and rubbers. 75 Main. Masonic Temple.

J. W. Neilly, Boots, shoes and rubbers, 26 Main, Eloskey building.

Louis Sendker, Dealer in boots and shoes. Fine custom work a specialty. Also repairing. 7 Pine.

B. Healy, Boot and shoe dealer. Also custom work. 4 Kennedy.

S. S. Levy, Boots and shoes, 82 Main.

I. Marks, Boots, shoes and trunks, 98 Main.

Racket Store, Boots, shoes and rubbers, 12 Kennedy.

BOOT AND SHOE MAKERS AND REPAIRERS.

G. Hogencamp, 147 Congress Ex.

W. H. Hudson, 388 East Main.

P. Wise, 84 Mechanic.

Jois Muscarell, 49 Mechanic.

P. H. De Straola, 9 Congress.

Nicola Scuteri, 18 Chambers.

R. L. Binney, 9½ Kennedy.

E. Reily, 4½ Kennedy.

Raffaele Suppo, 23 Davis.

G. Graff, 38 Webster.

F. L. Lordstrom, 46 Corydon.

Augustine Josberger, 42 Corydon.

Tony Mike, 51 Mechanic.

James Perkerell, 2 Roberts.

Sylvester Meyer, Custom work and repairing, 112 Washington.

Pascarella & Maio, 9 East Main.

L. L. Cetwick, 427 East Main.

B. Goodman, 82 Mechanic.

Mike Rich, 19 East Main.

Anthony Ciarlelli, 48 Brookline.

George Stewart, over 111 Main.

Mike Rich, 141 Main.

Rocco Curci, 75 Centre.

BOTTLERS.

Boston Bottling Company, D. Campbell, W. C. Maxwell, proprs. Manufacturers of all kinds of soda waters, birch beer and ginger ales, mineral waters and pure apple cider. Office and works, 29 Davis.

Independent Bottling Works, P. H. Davitt, propr.; John H. Douglas, mgr. Bottlers of beer, ale and porter. Sole agent for Vienna Cabinet Lager Beer. Office and works, 53 Mechanic. Tel. 118. Branch works at Limestone.

S. S. Woodbury, Bottler of lager beer, export beer, ale and porter. Bottles Bartholomay's Rochester Lager. Office and works, Mechanic, on West Branch Erie railroad. Tel. 195.

BOWLING ALLEYS.

Willard C. Wood, Three alleys, 10 Chambers.

BROKERS.

J. J. Freedley & Co., Brokers in stocks, grain and provisions. Room 21, Exchange Lyceum building, 35 Main. Tel. 59.

W. C. Higgins, Broker in New York and Chicago stocks, oil, grain and provisions. Over 51 Main. Tel. 26.

Moss Bros. (William E., George F.), Brokers in New York and Chicago stocks. Over 53 Main.

BUILDING AND LOAN ASSOCIATION.

Bradford Building and Loan and Savings Association, Authorized capital $1,000,000. George C. Fagnan, president; Robert Bauer, secretary General office, 6½ Main. Producers' Exchange. Telephone connection.

BUSINESS COLLEGE.

Bradford Business College, Joseph Leming, propr. An ideal American business school for both sexes. Day and evening sessions. Entire third floor Eloskey building, 24 Main.

CABINET MAKERS.

Claus Nelson, Cabinet maker and repairer. Repolishing and grilled work a specialty. 13 Barbour.

Graham Bros. (A. W., S. F.), Counters, shelving and fine cabinet work. Office and shops 4 Corydon. Tel. 214. (See contractors.)

Boss Brothers (F. W., J. B.), Fine Cabinet work and repairing of all kinds a specialty. Office and shop 106 Corydon.

CARRIAGE AND WAGON MANUFACTURERS.

Brown Bros. (J. E., C. B.), Carriage and wagon makers and repairers. All kinds of blacksmithing. 19-21 Pine.

M. B. Delmage, Carriage and wagon repairer and general blacksmith. 425 East Main.

C. L. Bookman, General carriage and wagon repairing. New work made to order. 147 Kendall ave.

M. B. Sanborn, Carriage and wagon repairing and general blacksmithing. 145 Kendall ave.

W. W. Penhollow, Wagon maker and house carpenter. Furniture repairing a specialty. 392 East Main.

F. E. Hinckley, Wagon and carriage repairing and general blacksmithing. 96-98 Washington.

John M. Green, Carriage and wagon repairing. 92 Corydon.

Armstrong Carriage Works, Established 1876. James McCleary, prop. Manufactures carriages and wagons. Repair work a specialty. First-class horseshoeing shop in connection. 2-4-6 Roberts.

Rogerson & Carlson (J. S. Rogerson, C. A. Carlson.), Carriage and wagon repairing. 33 Barbour.

Alexander Hilliker, Carriage and wagon repairing. 29 Barbour.

J. B. Callahan, Carriage and wagon repairing and general blacksmithing. 9 barbour.

S. G. Coffin, Manufacturer of and repairer of buggies and wagons. 6 Barbour. Tel. 136.

J. M. Englehaupt, Carriage and wagon repairing and general blacksmithing. . 26 Barbour.

H. Newell, Carriage and wagon repairing. Rear 5 Chestnut.

O'Brien Brothers (J. B. and E. H.), Carriage works. Repairing of all kinds. Rear 19 Bennett.

CARPET LAYERS.

John Alkins, 18 Pearl.

Geo. B. Brown, 17 Pine.

CARPET WEAVERS.

Cyrus Krepps, Weaves carpets, rugs and silk draperies. 35 Pearl, cor. Bank.

Mrs. R. Miller, Carpet weaving, 123 West Washington.

Mrs. J. B. Witman, Carpet weaving, 396 East Main.

Mrs. A. DuBois, rear 73 High.

CHARCOAL.

American Charcoal Co., M. B. Bubb, president, Williamsport, Pa.; C. F. Wright, vice president, Susquehanna, Pa.; R. .J. Gaffney, secretary and treasurer and general manager. Wholesale dealers in charcoal. Office, room 2, Bradburn block, 95 Main. Tel. 245.

CHIROPODISTS.

Louis Sendker, Surgeon chiropodist, 7 Pine.

A. J. Enty, 67 Corydon. Tel. 14-B.

Mrs. Jennie E. Thomas, Chiropodist and manicure. Hours 9 to 12 a. m. and 1:30 to 5:30 p. m. Room 12, Berry & Melvin block. 18 Main.

CHEMICAL WORKS.

Fuller Brook Chemical Works, Ph. Nusbaum, B. Nusbaum, Felix Streinberger, proprietors. Manufacturers of wood alcohol, acetate of lime, charcoal and wood tar. Works southwest of city on Fuller Brook. Office 5 Main. Tel.: Works, 209-B; office, 209.

The A. B. Smith Chemical Co., W. W. Smith, president; B. F. Hazelton, vice president; W. W. Bell, secretary and treasurer. Manufacturers of wood alcohol, acetate of lime and charcoal. Works on A. & K. Railway, west of city. Office, Room 3, Eloskey block, 24 Main. Tel.: Works 1, office 206.

Pennsylvania Tar Manufacturing Co., J. Wilkes Ford, president, Chicago, Ill.: John P. Sullivan, superintendent. Manufacturers of paving cement, roofing pitch, acetate of lime, wood alcohol and bituminous grout. Principal office at 731-733 South Ashland ave., Chicago. Works at 100 Davis. Tel. 11.

Lafayette Manufacturing Co., T. B. Clark, receiver. Manufacturers of wood alcohol, acetate of lime, etc. Works at Lewis Run, Erie and B. R. & P. Railways. Office 5 St. James. Tel. 128.

The Bradford Chemical Co., A. L. Wyman, president; J. C. Greenewald, secretary and treasurer. Works at Griffith Switch. Manufacturers of wood products. Office 124 Main.

Alton Chemical Co., J. C. Greenewald and A. L. Wyman, proprs. Works at Alton. Manufacturers of Wood products. Office 124 Main.

Gaffney, Arnold & Co., (W. S. and R. J. Gaffney, E. T. Arnold) Manufacturers of wood alcohol, acetate of lime, hardwood charcoal and tar. Principal office and works at Kushequa, Pa., Bradford office 95 Main, Bradburn block. Tel. 245.

National Chemical Co., W. S. Gaffney, president; R. J. Gaffney, secretary and treasurer. Manufacturers of wood alcohol. acetate of lime, hardwood charcoal and tar. Principal office and works at Kushequa, Pa. Bradford office 95 Main, Bradburn block. Tel 245.

CHINA, GLASS AND TINWARE.

W. D. Hatch, Two stores, 61 Main, 91 Mechanic.

J. B. Goodliff, 70 Mechanic.

Benjamin Rosenthal, 27 Main.

R. Hannahs, 393 East Main.

The Fair, 22 Main.

L. Emery, Jr., & Co., Plain and decorated China, Art Pottery, cut glass, electric and gas illuminating supplies. 43-45 Main. (See jewelry.)

CIGAR AND TOBACCO DEALERS.

H. B. Goe, 35 Main.

D. Whitestone, Wholesale and retail. 49 Main. Tel. 62.

Headlight Cigar Store, James Welsh, propr., 101 Main.

M. W. Albert, 4 Main.

B. F. Irvine, 63 Main.

J. A. Asselto, Wholesale and retail. 74 Main.

Wm. Boraird, Jr., 90 Main.

Nusbaum & Steinberger, 5 Main. Tel. 209.

M. F. Flaherty, Wholesale and retail. 1 Main. Tel. 270.

Bradford Stogie Co., Fred Miller, propr. Manufacturers of stogies and tobies. 12 Congress.

W. Stevens. 137½ Main.

Peter Burger, 177½ East Main.

CIGAR MANUFACTURERS.

H. Casterline, 35 Washington.

M. F. Flaherty, 56 Mechanic.

W. S. Keefe, Over 135 Main.

James Welsh, 101 Main.

Frank C. Dill, Cor. Winter and Centre.

Bradford Stogie Co., Fred Miller, propr. 12 Congress.

CIVIL ENGINEERS AND SURVEYORS.

J. A. Seymour, Over 6 Chambers.

F. M. Webster, 37 Corydon. Tel. 130-B.

A. F. Bannon, Jr., Assistant City Engineer. Room 9, over 48 Main.

P. .B Winfree, City Engineer. Room 9, over 48 Main. Tel. 299.

G. H. Lyon, 84 Corydon.

CLOTHING AND FURNISHINGS.

Temple Clothing Co., Fred Silberberg, propr. Clothing. Gents' furnishings, hats, caps, etc. 73 Main. Masonic Temple.

John B. Alden, C. M. Hooker, manager. Gents' furnishings. trunks, valises and clothing. 37 Main.

Ertz & Ertz (Sol. and J. M.), Clothing, furnishing goods, hats and caps, boots and shoes, trunks and valises. 29 Main.

Ellis Goodman, Clothing, gents' furnishing goods, boots and shoes, trunks and valises 133 Main.

A. R. Simons, Gents' furnishing goods. Sole agent for the Knox and Dunlap hats. 30 Main.

Marks' Clothing Co., M. Cohn propr. Clothing, gents' furnishings, trunks, etc. 47 Main.

Empire Clothing Co., G. E. Pitchford, manager. Custom and ready made clothing. Cash and installment plan. Cor. Main and Chambers, upstairs, Opera House block.

Misfit Clothing Parlors, M. A. Rosenberg, manager. G. F. Hoke, assistant manager. Merchant tailor-made garments exclusively. 56 Main.

H. Burlin, Clothing and gents' furnishings, 428-430 East Main.

Eitz & Joseph, (Izy Ertz, Abraham Joseph) Clothing, gents' furnishings, boots and shoes. 72-74 Mechanic.

The Racket Store, 6 to 14 Kennedy.

The Hub, I Brown, propr. Clothing and gents' furnishings. 104 Main.

Cash Clothing House, R. Michael, propr. Clothing exclusively. 120 Main.

Joseph Rothstein, Clothing and furnishings. 79 Washington.

S. Phillip, Clothing, gents' furnishings, boots and shoes. 54 Mechanic.

Greenewald's, (D. C. Greenewald, A. Silberberg) Clothing, hats and furnishings. 124 Main.

COAL AND WOOD.

W. Robinson, Dealer in coal and wood, lime, cement, fire brick, etc. 143 Main. Tel. 110-B.

COLLECTION AGENCY.

Commercial Collection Agency, W. J. Vallely, manager. 115½ Main.

CONFECTIONERY AND FRUIT.

Joe Onofrio, Confectionery, fruits cigars and tobaccos. 107 Main.

Greek-American Fruit Co., A. Mourzicon and P. Kaissmess, props Manufacturers and wholesale and retail dealers in confectionery. 44 Main.

Greek-American Fruit Co., John Constas, manager. Manufacturer of fine candies. Wholesale and retail dealers in confectionery, fruits and nuts. 28 Main.

G. Tammaro, Manufacturer and dealer in confectionery and ice cream. Fruits cigars and tobaccos. 78 Main.

J. B. Johnson, Confectionery, cigars, tobaccos and billiards. 181 East Main.

L. Loveless, Confectionery, cigars and tobacco. 105 East Main.

F. E. Winsor, Confectionery and cigars. 397 East Main.

John Healy, Confectiouery, fruits and cigars. 18 Congress.

Chris. Schneider, Confectionery, cigars. Lunch room attached. 99 Mechanic. Tel. 235.

J. F. Hubbard & Son, Manufacturers of ice cream and ices. 44 Davis. Tel 240.

W. A. Adamson, Manufacturer and wholesale and retail dealer in confectionery and ice cream. 138½ South Mechanic.

P. A. Allegrette, Manufacturer and wholesale and retail dealer in fine candies and ice creams. Headquarters for home made candies. Fruits, cigars and tobaccos. 73 Mechanic.

Weaver Brothers, R. A. Weaver, propr. Manufacturers of and wholesale dealers in candies and confections, and Jobbers in cigars. 9-11 Webster. Tel. 130-F. Retail branch store, fruits, confections and tobaccos. 105 Mechanic.

J. T. Shuckford, Candies, cigars and notions. 96 Rochester.

D. G. Lane, Confectionery, fruits, cigars and tobacco. 132 Main.

F. A. Bickford, Confectionery, cigars and tobacco, and stationery. 436 East Main.

Louis Ross, 115 Main.

Antonio Petillo, 66 Main.

R. Pope, 158 Main.

E. DeGoliers, 25 Davis.

Mrs. Mary Knowles, 43 Rochester.

CONTRACTORS AND BUILDERS.

John J. Lane, Contractor and builder. Plans and estimates furnished on application. Office 30 Boylston.

Peter McManus, Jr., Carpenter, contractor and builder, 112 Washington extension.

Breder & Brickell (Wm. H. Breder, Eli F. Brickell), Builders and contractors. Office 13 Phœnix block. 1 Main.

Boss Brothers (F. W., J. B.) Contractors and builders. Repairing of all kinds. Plans, specifications and estimates furnished on application. Office and shop 106 Corydon.

Graham Brothers (A. W., S. T.), Contractors and builders. Plans and estimates furnished on application. Office and shop 4 Corydon. Tel. 214.

E. N. Unruh, Contractor and builder Plans, estimates and specifications on application. Office, room 8 Phœnix block. 1 Main.

Chas. F. Cummings, Contractor and builder and general carpenter work. Office and shop 27 Barbour.

George W. Thornton, Contractor and builder. Repairing a specialty. Plans and estimates furnished. Rear 13½ Public Square.

William Hanley, Contractor and builder. Contract work exclusively. Plans and estimates furnished. Office at residence, 18 Jackson ave.

C. H. Merrow, Contactor and rig builder, 24½ Washington.

Frank McCarthy, Contractor. Stone work. 42 School.

J. T. Wilson, Contractor and builder. 44 Kennedy.

H. W. Bull, Contractor, carpenter and builder, 43½ Rochester.

John Dick, Contractor and builder. Mechanical draughtsman. 18 Patent alley.

Samuel D. Winters, Contractor and builder, 14 Pike.

John W. Baker, Contractor and builder. Stone and brick Masonry. 1 Clarence extension, off Sherman.

M. McMahon, Street paving, sewer and water line contractor. 32 Rochester.

J. R. McCarthy, Contractor. Stone and brick work. 109 Washington.

J. W. Hayes, Contractor and builder. Plans and estimates furnished. 15 Pine.

James Marshall, Contractor and builder. Third floor, 55 Main.

J. M. Hart, Contractor, carpenter and builder. 213 South Mechanic.

Z. Hill, Stone and brick mason and contractor. 11 Brookline.

W. H. Bannon, Stone mason and contractor. 9 Bennett.

John Sheehan, Street paving contractor. 5 Bank.

P. J. Purcell, Sidewalk contracton. 21 Mechanic.

David H. Fish, Carpenter, 39 Rochester.

DENTISTS.

Dr. C. M. Brooks, Room 1-3 Rosenberg & Michael block. 48 Main.

Dr. E. A. Hoenig, Room 3 Newell building. 102 Main.

Dr. W. P. Brinton, Crown bridge work a specialty. Rooms 6-7 Phœnix block. 1 Main.

Dr. W. W. Lewin, 85 Main.

Dr. A. B. Purdy, Crown bridge work a specialty. Bovaird & Seyfang block. 135 Main.

Dr. J. M. Crosby, Rooms 1-2 Eloskey building. 24 Main.

Dr. A. McAlpine, Room 8 Dikeman block. 34 Main.

DRESSMAKERS.

Mrs. S. Brown, Skirt making a specialty. 93 Boylston.

Mrs. F. F. Eisleben, 95 Boylston.

Miss Hattie Edmonds, 67 Foreman.

Mrs. R. D. Bareba, 77 Foreman.

Misses Bessie M. and Mary E. Farrer, 47 Foreman.

Mrs. Celia Tolman, 37 Foreman, cor. Florence.

Miss A. Perry, 31 Forman.

Miss E. J. Davidson, 10 Amm.

Mrs. K. Healy, 52 Kennedy.

Mrs. A. P. Leslie, Dressmaking and plain sewing, 15 Boylston.

Mrs. I. F. Watson, Fashionable dressmaking. Skirts and waists a specialty. 39 Davis.

Mrs. Mary Casey, Skirts a speciaty, 46 Davis.

Mrs. W. E. Hart, Skirts a specialty. 37 Davis.

Mrs. W. R. Fulmer, Specialty of cutting and fitting waists. 59 Chestnut.

Misses Barry (A. C., M. M.), 51 Chestnut.

Mrs. M. Mack, Cloak and Dressmaking. Also fur collarettes and repairing fur garments. Over 58 Corydon.

Miss Ella Buckinger, 22 Sherman.

Mrs. W. W. See, Dressmaking and plain sewing. 18 Jefferson.

Miss Mary J. Carruthers, 339 East Main.

Mrs. Cloe Simons, 313 East Main.

Mrs. Minnie Andress, Over 388 East Main.

Misses See & Hughes (Gertrude See, Nellie Hughes), Dress-making and children's clothes. Over 60 Main.

Miss J. L. Bissell, 69 Congress.

Mrs. C. Latshaw, Fashionable modiste and designer. All kinds of ladies' wear. A specialty of ladies' tailor-made garments, ball dresses, wedding trousseaus. Room 22 Producers Exchange, third floor. Public square.

Miss I. B. Howe, Over 23 Main.

Mrs. J. E. Conklin, Dressmaker and ladies' tailor. Rooms 7-8 Eloskey block. 24 Main.

Miss Ida McLain, Over 70 Mechanic.

Elizabeth Gardiner, Dress cutting and making. Tailor system. 2 Matteson.

Mrs. H. Lawrence, General dressmaking, 52 School.

Mrs. M. Miner, 79 State.

Mrs. A. V. son, 113 East Main.

Miss Nellie Davitt, 11 Park.

Julia A. **Cummings,** 23 Jefferson.

Miss Bid McKee, 62 Washington.

Miss Laura Wade, Over 115 Washington.

Mrs. Cornelia M. Burt, 54 High.

Miss Aurelia Perry, 31 Foreman.

Sarah E. **Campbell,** 5 Jefferson.

Miss Ellen M. Blossom, 99 Summer.

Mrs. A. Bascom, Modiste, 51 Corydon.

Miss Helen Bradley, 41 Congress.

Maria S. Winger, Rooms 1-4, Newell block. 100 Main.

Mrs. Susan Nesbitt, Over 122 Main.

Mrs. Julia Yerdon, Over 90 Main.

Miss Hanna Cantillon, 211 South Mechanic.

Mlle. L. M. La Chimner, Modiste. Cutting by McDowell system. Over 20 Main.

Mrs. Annie Lesh, 7 Kennedy.

Mrs. B. Videtto, 46 Chestnut.

DRILLERS AND CONTRACTORS.

J. H. Gayton, Oil, gas and water well contractor. Terms and estimates furnished on application. 291 East Main.

Oliver & Perkins (M. P. Oliver, A. A. Perkins), Contractors of artesian, water supply, gas and oil wells. Estimates furnished for drilling from 500 to 4,000 feet. 10 Petrolia.

S. J. Eginton, Contractor. Drilling and cleaning oil wells. Material furnished if desired. Office and residence, 12 Jerome ave.

N. J. Demming, Oil well contractor. Drilling, fishing, etc. 33 Walker ave.

A. D. BURNS,

PRACTICAL

Plumber, Gas and Steam Fitter.

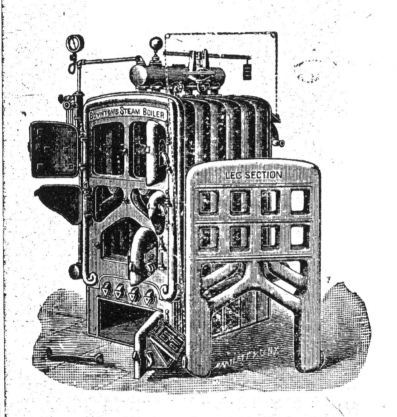

Hot Water Heating a Specialty.

14 Main Street, Bradford, Pa.

STERLING
CUSTOM TAILORING (

11 Main Street.

F. FREERKSON, PROPRIE

Suits and Overcoats Made to

AT POPULAR PRICES.

We carry the largest and and most complete line of fabrics for Suits and Overcoats to be found in Bradford.

Quality, fit, and workmanship guaranteed. Our clothes have style and finish. Goods made on the premises. It pays to wear our clothes.

STERLING CUSTOM TAILORING CO.,
F. FREERKSON, Proprietor.

Peter J. McMahon, Contractor. Oil well work, drilling, fishing and tool dressing. 43 Jackson ave.

Orran A. Knox, Contractor and driller. 8 Park.

C. J. Fitzgibbon, Expert tool fisher. Casing drawn by cutting, splitting or jarring. Removing casing damaged by nitro-glycerine a specialty. All kinds of fishing tools to rent. Residence and tool house, 21 Bank. Tel. 286.

William L. McVay, Oil well contractor and driller, 2 Washington.

E. S. Wilkinson, Contractor and driller, 155 Corydon.

James McAdoo, Oil well contractor and driller, 5 Jerome ave.

Perry J. Thayer, Oil well contractor and driller, 69 Bennett.

William T. Herrick, Driller and oil well contractor, 18 Bushnell.

William J. Hogan, Oil well contractor, 335 East Main.

DRUGGISTS.

Thompson & Wood, (E. K. Thompson, F. D. Wood) 19 Main. Tel. 273.

W. O. Neely, 85 Main. Tel. 247.

C. V. Cottrell (Successor to Davis & Cottrell), 95 Main. Tel. 148.

Fagnan & Green (Geo. C. Fagnan, Chas. Green), 117 Main. Tel. 175.

E. P. Southwick & Co., 34 Main. Tel. 140.

W. D. Hart, 13 Main. Tel. 278-B.

H. A. Van Voris, 160 Main.

D. F. Hart, 434 East Main.

E. E. Clark, 424 East Main.

John C. Calhoun & Son, 412 East Main. Public Tel.

J. F. Leonard, 78 Mechanic.

Callender's Drug Store, W. B. Callender, propr. 109 Mechanic. Phoenix block. Tel. 207-B.

DRY GOODS, CLOAKS, CARPETS.

The Bazaar, Julius Eloskey, propr. Dry goods, cloaks, millinery and house furnishing goods. 24 Main, Eloskey building.

The Fair, R. Rosenberg, propr. Department store. Dry goods, millinery, shoes and slippers, boys' clothing, crockery, etc., etc. 22 Main.

Cohn Bros. (Isaac, Archie D.), Dry goods, cloaks and ladies' furnishings, 20 Main.

T. B. Brown, Dry Goods, carpets, cloaks and millinery. Millinery department on second floor. 93 Main.

Robert B. Johnston, Dry goods, millinery, cloaks and ladies' fine furnishings, 53 Main.

J. Kreinson, Dry goods. cloaks. ladies' furnishings and notions. Also carpet store in connection. Portieres. rugs, draperies, etc. 100-102 Main.

S. Auerbaim, Dry goods, fancy goods and cloaks. 48 Main.

H. Burlin, Dry goods and ladies' furnishings, 428-430 East Main.

H. Boyer, Dry goods, boots and shoes. 398 East Main.

S. Phillip, Dry goods and clothing, 54 Mechanic.

Ertz & Joseph. Dry goods. cloaks. ladies' furnishings, etc 72-74 Mechanic. (See clothing.)

S. Brand. Dry goods and ladies' and gents furnishings. 11-13 Kennedy.

Racket Store, O. C. Stewart. propr. Dry goods, cloaks and ladies' furnishings. 8 to 14 Kennedy.

D. O'Donnell, Dry goods. millinery, and notions, 36 Main.

"Bell" Dry Goods Company, Dry goods. cloaks. ladies' and children's furnishings, 18 Main, cor. Public Square.

Joseph Rothstein, Ladies' furnishings and dry goods, 79 Washington.

Sloan & Ervin, Carpets, 16 Public Square. (See Furniture.)

DYERS.

The Queen City Dye Works, C. M. Gage & Sons. proprs. General cleaning, dyeing and repairing. 84 Boylston.

Keystone Steam Dye Works, W. E. Johnson, propr. Ladies' and gentlemen's garments dyed, cleaned and repaired. 89 Mechanic.

Bradford Steam Dye Works. Hugh Stinson and Edward Edwards. proprs. Cleaning and dyeing ladies' and gentlemen's clothes. 13 Chestnut.

Mrs. M. J. Brayton, Cleaning. repairing and dyeing ladies and gents' wearing apparel. Over 61½ Main.

S. M. Cohen, Dyeing, tailoring, cleaning and repairing 84 Mechanic.

D. F. Moriarty, Dyeing, cleaning and repairing men's garments. 111 Main.

Harry Bryman, Dyeing, cleaning and repairing. 11 Washington..

ELECTRICAL SUPPLIES.

E. E. McQuiston, 66 Chestnut.

E. E. Buel, 35 Main.

ELECTRICIANS.

L. Sheehan, Room 20, Exchange Lyceum, 35 Main.

George W. Smith, 48 Elm.

E. C. Timberly, Telephone Exchange, over 53 Main.

EXPRESS COMPANIES.

American Express Co., F. A. McKenzie, manager. 79 Main. Tel. 25.

Wells, Fargo & Co., E. B. Thomas, Agent. 85 Main. Tel. 47.

———

FLOUR AND FEED MILLS.

Terrell Bros., 38 Mechanic. (See grocers.) Tel. 219.

W. N. Hanna, Near junction Jackson and Seward avenues, on Erie Railroad. Tel. 116-Y.

C. L. Douglass, Flour and feed mills, foot Mill street, East Bradford.

FISH MARKETS.

W. J. Long, Fresh and salt water fish, oysters, clams and game is season. 80 Mechanic.

J. Rogalsky, Fresh and salt water fish, poultry and oysters in season. 6 Chambers.

J. Singer, Fish and poultry market. 26 Pearl.

FLORISTS.

Milton I. Deuel, Cut flowers, pot plants, palms, etc. Funeral designs, decorations, etc. Greenhouses, 141 to 149 Congress extension. Tel. 138-B. Office, 22 Congress. Tel. 287.

W. C. Rockwell, Cut flowers and potted plants. Funeral work a specialty. Office and store, 13 Main, Exchange Lyceum. Tel. 99. Greenhouse, Washington extension.

George L. Graham, Decorations and floral work a specialty. Cut flowers always on hand. Greenhouses, 58 Seward ave., East Bradford. Office and store, 87 Main. Tel. 116-W.

G. R. Oliver, Cut flowers and potted plants. A specialty of carnations and Chrysanthemums. Ferns and palms. Greenhouses, 3 Pleasant and 106 Washington. Downtown office, 1 Main. Tel. 270.

Oak Hill Florist, M. A. Tugwell. Office and greenhouses, East Main, at entrance to Oak Hill Cemetery.

FLOUR AND FEED DEALERS.

See Grocers.

FURNITURE DEALERS.

Sloan & Ervin, (James M. Sloan, Elmer L. Ervin), Furniture, carpets, rugs, fine bric-a-brac, etc. 16 Public Square. Tel. 106-B.

D. T. Drew, Furniture, etc. 45 Boylston. Orpheus hall.

J. M. Burchfield, New and second-hand furniture and stoves. 19-21-23 Chestnut.

GAS AND ELECTRIC LIGHT COMPANIES.

Commercial Natural Gas Co., E. W. Lewis, treasurer and manager. Fuel and illuminating. 112 Mechanic, St. James block. Tel. 266.

Manufacturer's Gas Co., T. N. Barnsdall, president, E. P. Whitcomb, vice president, Wm. Barnsdall, Jr., secretary and treasurer. Fuel and illuminating. Office 15 Chautauqua Place. Tel. 277.

Glen Hazel Gas Co., R. E. Powers, secretary and treasurer. Office 24 Congress. Tel. 292.

United Natural Gas Co., W. C. Henry, superintendent. Office 69-71 Main. Tel. 215.

Bradford Electric Light & Power Co., George H. Potter. president, J. H. Rose, general manager. Light and power. Office and works 48-50 Chestnut. Tel. 230.

GROCERS.

Nusbaum & Steinberger (Bennett Nusbaum, Felix Steinberger), Wholesale and retail. Groceries, provisions, flour, feed, hay, oats, straw, etc. 3-5 Main. Tel. 209.

Blossom & Toy (H. S. Blossom, W. H. Toy). Groceries, provisions, flour, feed, hay, oats straw, etc. 113 Main. Tel. 122.

J. A. Waldo, Flour, feed, hay, oats and straw exclusively. Rear 115 Main.

W. H. Oxley, Fancy and staple groceries, 86 Main. Tel. 150.

L. A. Fischer & Co. (L. A. Fischer, Joseph Fischer), Groceries, provisions, flour. feed, hay, oats, straw, etc. 92 Main. Tel. 229.

M. H. Hughes, Fancy and staple groceries and feed, 116 Main. Tel. 133.

W. C. Palmer & Co., Wholesale and retail. Groceries, flour, feed, hay, oats and straw. 128-130 Main. Tel. 177.

Paul & Leyman, (J. G. Paul, Wm. H. Layman), Fancy and staple groceries, flour, hay and feed. 156 Main. Tel. 106.

Smith Brothers, (S. H., F. L.), Wholesale and retail. Groceries, provisions, flour, feed, hay, oats, straw, etc. Store 9 Main. Warehouse cor. Brookline & Centre. Tel. 167.

Terrell Bros., (S. A., L. A.), Wholesale and retail. Groceries, provisions, flour, feed, hay, oats and straw. Feed mill 38 Mechanic. Store cor. Washington and Pearl. Tel. 219.

Slack & Morrow, (Frank E. Slack, John E. Morrow), Groceries and provisions. Tobacco and cigars. 179 East Main. Tel. 259-W.

O. F. Spencer, Wholesale and retail. Groceries and provisions, hay oats and straw. 401-403 East Main. Tel. 116.

I. D. Brown, Groceries and provisions, flour, feed, hay and straw. 471-473 East Main.

H. Burlin, Groceries, provisions, flour, feed, hay. oats and straw. 428-430 East Main.

J. C. Smith, Groceries and provisions, flour, feed, hay, oats and straw. 426 East Main.

Fred H. Leroy, Groceries and provisions, flour and feed, hay, oats and straw. Cor. Washington and Mechanic. Tel. 145.

Maltby & Freeman. Grocers, 108 Summer, cor. Jackson ave. and Pleasant. Tel. 57.

S. Fisher, Groceries, 20 Pearl.

C. G. Fritts, Fancy and staple groceries, 63 Mechanic.

The Family Grocery House, M. A. Nusbaum, propr. Groceries and provisions. 67 Mechanic.

L. M. Brink, Groceries, 141 Congress extension.

Loveless & Schiewe (N. J. Loveless, A. A. Schiewe), Groceries and provisions, hay. flour and feed. 31-33 Kennedy, cor. Boylston, opp. City Hall. Tel. 173.

E. L. Caskey & Son, Groceries. Cor. Jefferson and Leland avenue.

Howard Andrews, F. W. Agnew, manager. Groceries and provisions. 43 Pearl.

R. P. Hinman. Groceries. flour, provisions etc. 97 Washington.

Nutting & Hopkins (L. Nutting, A. Hopkins), Groceries, flour, feed, etc. 71 Washington.

H. Cohn, Groceries, provisions and stationery. 51 Washington.

A. D. Hervey, Groceries and provisions. Home-made bread pies and cakes. 49 Washington.

Ben H. Green, Myrom Johnson, manager. General store. Groceries. flour, feed and hay. Main office at Allegany, N. Y. Store 37 Washington.

J. H. Roche, Groceries and provisions 44 School.

Nichols & McClintock (A. D. Nichols, H. S. McClintock), Groceries and provisions, hay, feed, oats and straw. Cor. Corydon and Mechanic. Tel. 278.

Peterson & Bachman (J. A. Peterson, C. Bachman), Groceries and provisions, fruits and vegetables. 95 Mechanic. Tel. 235-3.

B. C. Caterina, Groceries and provisions, teas. coffees and spices, tobacco and cigars. 75 Mechanic.

Hermiss & Son (Dominic and Henry J.), Groceries and provisions, cigars and tobacco. 11 Pine.

D. S. Loveless, Groceries and provisions, Mocha and Java coffees and Mrs. Seeley's home-made bread. 153 Jackson ave.

C. H. Denninger, Groceries and provisions, teas and coffees, flour, feed, hay, etc. 54 Davis, cor. Foreman.

L. M. Wynkoop, Groceries and provisions, fresh and smoked meats. 6 Brennan.

G. G. Bennett, Groceries and provisions. Pillsbury's best flour. Cor. Chambers and Corydon. Tel. 218-B.

Kiva Berwald, Groceries, provisions and smoked meats, 33 Bushnell.

J. H. Rhinehart, Groceries and provisions. 46 Brookline.

Boyle & Williams (E. J. Boyle, G. D. Williams), Groceries and provisions. Teas, coffees and spices, flour and feed. Also retail and wholesale dealers in maple sugar and syrup. 71 Congress. Tel. 217.

A. D. Moulton, Wholesale and retail groceries and provisions. Flour, feed, hay and straw. 437 East Main.

L. Pitkin & Son, Staple and fancy groceries and provisions. 161 Main.

H. Boyer, Groceries and general store. 398 East Main.

T. Young, 88 Washington.

S. Orange. 5 Pearl and 14 Congress.

A. P. McConnell, 23 Main.

GUN AND LOCKSMITHS.

G. R. Mabb, Gun and locksmith and generaal repairing. Manufactures rubber stamps, stencils, seals, badges, etc. Umbrellas repaired and re-covered. 7 Congress.

H. A. Harvey, Guns, bicycles, sporting goods and general repairing, 113 Main.

H. Casterline, Lock and gunsmith and general jobbing and repairing, 35 Washington.

HAIRDRESSERS AND HAIR DEALERS.

Miss M. May Wicks, Hair dressing and manicuring. Room 9. Dikeman block, over 36 Main.

Mrs. J. Maurer, Manufacturer of and dealer in hair goods, 84 Main, upstairs.

Mrs. M. A. Holmes, Hair dressing parlors. Steam baths, manicuring, all-over massage. Toilet articles of all kinds for sale. 6 Janes Place.

Mrs. Mary J. Donohue, Manufacturer of and dealer in hair goods. Agent for the Buffalo Corset. 12 Congress, upstairs.

Miss E. Keenan, Hair goods, over 3 Webster.

Mrs. W. W. See, Ladies' hair work, 18 Jefferson.

HARDWARE.

M. A. Haggerty, General hardware and housefurnishing goods, farming implements. 415 East Main.

The Great Supply House (L. Emery, Jr., W. R. Weaver), Dealers in hardware, stoves and ranges. Granite and tinware. Refrigerators, bicycles, baby carriages, carpet sweepers, paints, oils and glass. 43-45 Main. Tel. 274.

George A. Bodine, Hardware, stoves and ranges, tin and granite ware. Baby carriages and refrigerators, paints, oils and glass. 98-100 Mechanic. Tel. 232.

J. B. Fox, Hardware, stoves and tinware. Builders' hardware and general housefurnishings. Sole agent for the Pittsburg gas heating stoves. 60 Main and 2-4 Chestnut. Tel. 111.

T. M. Griffith & Son, Hardware, stoves, ranges and refrigerators. Tinware and sheet metal workers. 165 Main, cor. East Main. Tel. 122-B.

HARNESS MAKERS AND DEALERS.

M. L. Pomeroy, Manufacturer of harness and dealer in all kinds of horsefurnishing goods. Whips, blankets, robes, saddles, etc. 6 Pine.

C. Wagner, manufacturer of light and heavy harness and collars, and dealer in horse furnishing goods. Repairing a specialty. 5-7 Kennedy.

L. Emery, Jr., & Co., Harness, blankets and horse furnishings. 43-45 Main. (See hardware.)

J. P. Whittlesey, Harness manufacturer and dealer in light and heavy harness, whips, blankets, robes, etc. 417 East Main.

HAT MANUFACTURER.

D. F. Moriarty, Manufacturer of men's stiff, silk and soft hats. Hats made to order. 111 Main.

HORSESHOERS.

John M. Green, 92 Corydon.

H. F. Farnsworth, Horseshoeing exclusively. 15 Webster.

Rogerson & Carlson, 33 Barbour.

Alexander Hilliker, Contracted feet a specialty. 29 Barbour.

Sam Stoffer, Practical horseshoeing. 9 Pine.

J. B. Callahan, 9 Barbour.

J. M. Englehaupt, 26 Barbour.

F. E. Hinckley, 96-98 Washington.

M. B. Delmage, 423 East Main.

M. B. Sandborn, 145 Kendall ave.

James McCleary, 2-4-6 Roberts.

H. Newell, Horseshoeing. Rear 5 Chestnut.

HOTELS.

The Option House, American and European plan. Sea food a specialty. Game in season. 39 Main. Tel. 263.

The Imperial, American and European plans. 75 Main, Tel. 265.

The Vienna Cafe and Hotel, J. C. Weaver, propr., 81-83 Main, Tel. 152.

The Riddell House, F. P. Holley, propr. Rates, $2.00 and $2.50 per day, Cor. Main and Davis. Tel. 262.

The Rochester, William Devine, propr. Rates, $1.50 and $2.00 per day. 155 Main, opp. B., R. & P. depot. Tel. 187.

The New Bay State, A. E. Hurley. propr. Rates, $2.00 per day. 72-74 Main. Tel. 133-F.

Oil City House, Otto Gash. propr. Rates, $1.00 per day. 106-108 Main. Tel. 180.

Willard Hotel, W. K. Urquhart, propr., 116-118-120 Main.

Union House, Fred Heckel, propr., 126 Main.

St. James Hotel, J. C. Fox, propr., Rates, $2.00 and $2.50 per day. Public Square. Head Main. Tel. 261.

Mansion House, P. Mulqueen, propr. Rates, $2.00 per day. 104-106 Mechanic.

The United States Hotel, G. A. Crooker, propr. Rates, $1.50 per day. 88-90 Mechanic. Tel. 195-B.

Tuna Valley House, Edward Ryan and P. A. Keane, props., 411 East Main.

American House, P. M. White, propr. Rates, $1.00 per day. 440 East Main.

The Conneely, Thomas Connelly. propr. Rates. $1.00 per day. 93 Mechanic.

The Black Bear, M. Herron, propr. Rates, $1.25 per day. 8 to 16 Pine. Tel. 275.

Corry House. P. McNamara, propr. Rates, $1.00 per day. 10-12 Webster.

Washington House, Jas. H. Burns, propr. 6-8 Webster. Tel. 189.

Henderson House, M. E. Hildebrand, propr Rates, $1.00 per day. Cor. Corydon and Webster. Tel. 155.

Aiken House, Eugene Peake, propr. Rates, $1.00 per day. 108-110 Washington. Tel. 225.

The Industry, L. A. Coleman & Co. (Clyde M. McDonell.) Rates, $1.00 per day. 17-19 Davis. Tel. 259-F.

Pierce House, P. J. Hennessy, propr. 107-109 Main.

ICE DEALERS.

Bradford Ice Company (J. J. Sheehy, H. Boss). Office, 110 Mechanic. Tel. 224.

C. L. Baker, Office and Ice Houses at Bolivar Run.

INSTALLMENT HOUSE.

American Wringer Company, James D. Riley, manager. Wringers and household specialties. Office room, 1, Newell block, 102 Main.

INSURANCE.

The Prudential Life Insurance Company, of Newark. N. J. J. W. Hannan, assistant superintendent. Office, 14 Phœnix block, 1 Main.

Vermont Life Insurance Company, of Burlington. Vt., A. R. Porter, superintendent. Office, 11 Phœnix block 1 Main.

The Metropolitan Life Insurance Company, of New York, Thomas Conroy, assistant superintendent. Office, 5 Phœnix block, 1 Main.

The Penn Mutal Life Insurance Company, of Philadelphia, Pa., Harry F. West, president; Henry C. Brown, secretary and treasurer. Assets, $29,405,529.08; surplus, $3,-594,126.79. Costello Brothers (J. L. and T. E.), general agents, Office, 110 Mechanic, cor. Public Square. Tel. 224.

C. H. Kennedy, Fire, life and accident insurance, 53 Main, up stairs.

Paton & Wheeler (George Paton, Charles L. Wheeler, Jr.), Fire, life, accident and plate glass insurance, 59 Main. Tel. 3.

Robert Bauer, Fire, life, accident and plate glass insurance, 6 Public Square, Producers' Exchange building. Tel. 174.

New York Life Insurance Company, John A. McCall, president. Assets, $187,174.406; surplus, $26,657,332. A. F. Danilson, general agent. Office, 1 Congress. Tel. 125.

George W. Funk, Fire, life and accident insurance. Office in Dikeman block, over 36 Main.

E. V. Cody, Life and accident, 83 Corydon.

Employers' Liability Assurance Corporation, Ltd., of London, England. Capital, $5,000,000. A. F. Danilson, agent, 1 Congress. Tel. 125.

Central Accident Insurance Company, of Pittsburg, Pa. Capital, $100,000; surplus, $100,000. Accident and plate glass insurance. Costello Bros., general agents. 110 Mechanic. Tel. 224.

Safety Fund Insurance, R. W. Murray, district commander. Office, 1 Nickel Plate block, 111 Main.

Home Life Insurance Company, of New York. W. M. Murray, city agent. Office, 1 Nickel Plate block, 111 Main.

New England Mutual Life Insurance Company, Burnett S. Love, agent, 11 Kane.

IRON, BRASS AND STEEL WORKS.

Tuna Iron Works, Frank Hamilton, proprietor; W. T. Elliott, manager. Manufactures drilling tools. Office and works 61-63 Elm. Tel. 282. Branch stores at Pittsburg, Pa., and Sistersville, W. Va.

D. Phillips & Co., A. Laley, general manager. Manufacturers of drilling and fishing tools. Office and works 87 Chestnut. Tel. 176.

D. W. Robertson, Manufactures drilling and fishing tools. Blacksmith and machine shop. 104-106 Chestnut.

Bovaird & Seyfang Manufacturing Co., O. D. Bleakley, president; J. E. Ward, secretary and treasurer; J. E. Cochran, general manager. Manufacturers of oil, gas and artesian well supplies, boilers, engines, stills, retorts, refining equipments, oil well wood work. A specialty of gas and steam engines. Also contractor's and builder's supplies of every description.

Bradford works on Davis, Boylston, Foreman and Hilton streets. Number people employed in Bradford works 200. Works also at 546 Second avenue, Pittsburg, Pa. Stores at Butler, Pa., Sistersville, W. Va., Parkersburg, W. Va., and South Vandalia, N. Y. Principal office at Bradford, Pa., 30 Davis. Tel. 164.

Close & Caldwell (R. M. Close, E. R. Caldwell), manufacturers of engines, rig irons, oil well supplies, iron and brass castings of all descriptions. Manufacturers of the celebrated "C and C" engines. Repair work a specialty. Capacity of foundry, three tons daily. Number employed, 25. Office and works, cor. Erie Railway and Newell ave. Tel. 183.

Locke Machine Works, F. A. Fowler, propr., H. H. Locke, manager, Brass and iron founders. Machine and blacksmith work to order. Repair work a specialty. Capacity of foundry, two tons per day. Number employed, 15. Office and works, 25 to 35 Webster, cor. Corydon. Tel. 214-B.

Bradford Tool Works, John Ley, propr., manufacturers of oil well tools and general repairing. Fishing tools of all kinds to let. Number employed, 10. Office and works, 30 to 34 Corydon. Tel. 258.

O'Brien & Double (P. O,Brien, G. W. Double), Practical boiler makers. Dealers in second-hand boilers. Repair work a specialty. 25 Barbour.

S. R. Dresser, Patentee and manufacturer of oil and gas well packers, pipe couplings and clamps. Office and works, 15 Patent alley, rear 61 Main.

The McElwaine Company, Ltd., C. P. Collins, chairman; W. M. Kincaid, secretary and treasurer. Manufacturers of the Hoadley improved wall and anchor packers for oil, gas and artesian wells. Agents for Allison's tubing, casing and drive pipe. General machine shop. Works, 7 Railroad, cor. Newell avenue. Tel. 135-B. Office, room 10, Exchange Lyceum. Tel. 295.

B., R. & P. Railroad Shops, A. Bardsley, master mechanic; P. C. Rusch, general foreman. Overhauling and repairing of engines for company's use. Employing 200 men. Office and shops located on B., R. & P. R. R., south of city. Tel. 243-B.

B., B. & K. Railroad Shops, Charles Greenough, master mechanic. Overhauling and repairing of engines and rolling stock for company. Shops on Thompson ave. and railroad.

Oil Well Supply Company, John Eaton, president; K. Chickering, vice president; Louis Brown, treasurer; E. T. Howes, general treasurer; K. Saulnier, assistant treasurer; J. C. Palmer, secretary. Manufacturers of all kinds of oil and gas well supplies. Complete outfits ready for drilling, and everything necessary for the producing of oil or natural gas. Mills at Pittsburg, Pa., for the manufacture of wrought iron pipe, also machine and blacksmith shop. Works at Oil City for the manufacture of engines and all kinds of wrought iron work used in the oil business. At Van Wert, Ohio, a saw mill and sucker rod factory. At

Bradford, Pa., machine and boiler shop, 28-30-32-34 Mechanic. Rig, reel and wheel factory, 10-12-14-16-18 Davis. Stores at Pittsburg, Pa., Harmony, Pa., Mars, Pa., Washington, Pa., McDonald, Pa., Evans City, Pa., Kane, Pa., 29 Church street, New York city, Bolivar, N. Y., Fostoria, O., Lima, O., Marietta, O., Montpelier, Ind., Alexandria, Ind., Peru, Ind., Parkersburg, W. Va., Sistersville, W. Va., Waverly, W. Va, and Cairo, W. Va. Bradford store 94 Main cor. Webster. Tel. 115. Principal offices 94 Main. Cable address, "Eatonoil."

JEWELRY AND BRIC-A-BRAC.

Brennan & Davis, Jewelry, silverware, bric-a-brac, pictures and art goods. 21 Main. (See booksellers and stationers.)

L. Emery, Jr., & Company, Watches, clocks and diamonds. Jewelry, silverware and novelties, Bric-a-brac and art goods. 43-45 Main. (See hardware.)

P. L. Lowenthal, Watches, diamonds, silverware and fancy goods. 65 Main.

M. A. De Golier, Jewelry and optician. Diamonds, watches, cut glass and novelties. Cor. Main and Kennedy.

J. B. Cross, Jeweler and optician. Fine watch repairing. 91 Main.

C. C. Coats, Jeweler and optician. Watch and clock repairing a specialty. 115½ Main.

Matthews & Lancey (J. T. Matthews, George H. Lancey), Jewelry and silverware. Watch, clock and jewelry repairing a specialty. 121 Main.

Opera House Jewelry Store, B. F. Rothstein, propr. Watches, clocks, jewelry, silverware and musical merchandise. 54 Main, Opera House block.

W. L. Field, Jewelry, watches, etc. Watch and clock repairing. 110 Main (See booksellers and stationers.)

P. T. Shirkey, Watchmaker and jeweler. Engraving a specialty. 388 East Main.

A. M. Selden, Jeweler. Watch, clock and jewelry repairing 52 Mechanic.

L. C. Bullard, Watchmaker. Watch and clock repairing of all kinds. 21 Congress.

S. Werthman, Watchmaker. Watch and clock repairing. 84 Main.

Rothstein & Lippman Bros., 7 Main.

LAUNDRIES.

Bradford Steam Laundry, J. J. Freeman and L. M. Kathan, proprs. First class laundry. Work of all descriptions done on short notice. Lace curtains, carpet cleaning and dye work a specialty. Employes 35 people. Main office and works, 11 to 19 Bishop. Tel. 125-B. City office, 1 Congress. Tel. 125.

City Steam Laundry, C. W. Baker, propr. A specialty of fine fabrics of all kinds in addition to regular laundry work. 27 Pine. Tel. 103-B.

Crosiers' Steam Laundry, George W. Crosier, propr. All work done by hand. 42 Boylston.

Hornellsville Steam Laundry, Ben Toy, agent, 3 Howard Place. Tel. 44-B.

Dunkirk Steam Laundry, H. H. Messimer, agent, 71 school.

LEATHER AND FINDINGS.

John Meyers, Dealer in leather and findings. Also manufacturer of shoe uppers. 13 Corydon.

LIQUOR DEALERS.

N. R. Collins & Co., (Frank J. Collins), Wholesale, wines, liquors and cigars. Proprietors of Gold Leaf Distilling Co. Distillers of gold leaf rye whiskies. 88 Main. Tel 109.

Louis Marck, Wholesale wines, liquors, cigars and tobacco. Co-operative and export beers. 122 Main Tel. 188.

H. M. Plague, Wholesale dealer in wines, liquors and cigars. Sole agent for J. H. Cutter and McKean club rye whiskies. 108 Mechanic. Tel. 225-B.

Bear Fordonski, Wholesale dealer in fine wines and liquors. Tobacco and cigars. Family trade a specialty. 84 Main.

A. Mayer & Co., Established in 1876. (A. Mayer & M. Rolland.) Wholesale dealers in wines, liquors, cigars and tobaccos. Sole agents for McKean county for Bartholomay's Rochester beer. Also agents for Beck's Brewing Co.'s Buffalo beer. 114 Main. Tel. 193.

LIVERY AND BOARDING STABLES.

George B. Weaver, Livery, boarding and feed stable. 33-35 East Main. Tel. 168-B.

A. F. Moore, Boarding, livery and feed stable. 9 Chambers and 10 Chestnut. Tel. 181.

Walter Grubb, Boarding and livery stable. 19 Kennedy. Tel. 139.

N. M. Thompson, Livery, boarding and feed stable. 14 Corydon.

Henderson House Barn, Ira Haskins, propr. Livery, boarding and feed stable. 26 Corydon. Tel. 155.

W. M. Crandall, Boarding and livery stable, 421 East Main.

A. D. Moulton, Boarding and livery stable, 439 East Main.

Charles F. Newton, Livery, boarding and feed stable. 135-137 Mechanic. Tel. 185.

S. G. Coffin, Livery, boarding and feed stables. Barns at 8-10-12 Barbour. Tel. 136. 13½ Congress. Tel. 136-B. 73 Main, rear Masonic Temple. Tel, 136-F.

Rochester Hotel Barn, William Devine, propr. Feed, board and transient stables. 8-10 Roberts.

LUMBER.

J. M. Bemis & Son (Harry C.). manufacturers and wholesalers of hemlock lumber. Office, 7 Producers' Exchange building, Public Square. Tel. 165.

B. F. Hazelton, manufacturer and wholesale and retail dealer in lumber. Office and yards, 33 North Mechanic. Tel. 255.

P. A. Kent, Dealer in lumber, sash, doors and Glass, 36 Mechanic. Tel. 220-B.

W. S. Weed & Co. (W. S. and Charles Weed and S. A. Munday), Lumber manufacturers. Hemlock and hardwood lumber. Mills at Glen Charles, Pa. Office, 124 South Mechanic, Pompelon Hall, Tel. 160.

A. J. Bond, Wholesale dealer in high grades of hardwood and hemlock lumber, lath and shingles. Office, 124 South Mechanic, Pompelon Hall. Tel. 114.

Stout & Holden (A. A. Stout, A. C. Holden), Manufacturers of hemlock and hardwood lumber. Mill at Sugar Run. Tel. at mill 169. Office, over 83 Main. Tel. 240-B.

Tuna Manufacturing Co. (W. H. Dennis, W. A. Benjamin, W. A. Warner, proprietors.), Lumber dealers and general building contractors. Office and store fixtures, wood mantels, tile, hearths and facings. Mill and office Mechanic and West Branch Erie Railway. Tel. 220.

A. Miller & Son (Fred A.) Manufacturers and dealers in all kinds of lumber, doors, sash, blinds, glass, etc. Builders' supplies of every description. 86 Kennedy. Tel. 141.

Howard Andrews, Wholesale dealer in lumber. Office 84 Davis. Tel. 226.

J. R. Droney Lumber Co., Wholesale manufacturers and dealers in hemlock, hardwood and pine lumber, shingles and lath. Mills at Underwood, Pa., and Taintor, Pa., on Erie railroad; Gerald, Pa., on B., R. & P. Railroad, and Lemings, Pa , on B. B. & K. Railroad. Office at Olean, N. Y., Temple building. Bradford office, Room 20, Davis block, over 21 Main. Tel. 234.

MANUFACTORIES.

Dresser & Booth (S. R. Dresser George P. Booth), manufacturers of sucker rods, 15 Patent Alley.

Alumina Shale Brick Company, C. P. Collins, president; C. V. Merrick, vice president; T. J. Melvin, secretary, treasurer and general manager; J. P. Melvin, assistant secretary and treasurer. Manufacturers of pressed brick of all kinds. Works at Lewis Run, Pa. Office, 3 Berry & Melvin block, 18 main. Tel. 192.

T. W. Roberts, Manufacturer and dealer in wooden tanks, 154 Main.

Bradford Enameling Company, W. W. Bell, president; W. W. Smith, vice president; J. P. Melvin, secretary and treasurer; T. J. Melvin, general manager. Manufacturers of enameled brick. Works at Lewis Run. Office, 3 Berry & Melvin block, 18 Main. Tel. 192.

Pompelon Glass Works, William Andrews King, secretary and general manager. Manufacturers of crvstal green bottles, demijohns, flasks, etc. Works on Erie railroad. near Hilton. Office, Pompelon Hall, Public Square. Tel. 219-B.

Bradford Planing Mill Company, D. W. Frazee, propr. Manufactures sash, doors, blinds, etc. Office and mill, 84 Davis. Tel. 226.

Morrison & Co. (C. S. Morrison, Robert Bishop), Manufacturers of sash and doors, and dealers in glass. 54 Chestnut. Tel. 107-B.

Medical Gum Company (E. W., W. W., J. J. & C. F. Bisett), Manufacturers of "The Doctor" and Pepsin chewing gum. Office and factory, 19 Webster. Tel. 214.

Bradford Paint Company, W. N. Tryon, propr. Manufacturer of paints. 11 Corydon.

Bedell & Crouse, Alva A. Bedell, propr.; James H. Bedell, superintendent. Manufacturers of bundle kindling wood Capacity, 16 cars a week. Employing 110 people. Principal office, 169-171 Third street, Jersey City, N. J. Office and works on B., R. & P. railroad, foot Fisher ave., East Bradford. Tel. 75-B.

Durham & Sweesy (E. A. Durham, T. Sweesy), Manufacturers of and dealers in "Sweesy's Patent Ink Well." 57 Pearl.

Fairbanks-Boston Rim Co., Lewis Emery. Jr., president; H. C. Wilcox, secretary; W. G. Webber, treasurer; B. M. Bailey, assistant treasurer and general manager. Manufacturers of wood rims, mud and chain guards. Capacity, 1,250,000 rims and 200,000 mud and chain guards per year. Employing 125 people. Operating three plants, situated at Bradford, Pa., Bedford, Mass., and Toronto, Canada. Total number employed 500 people. Principal office and works at Bradford, Pa., cor. Jackson ave. and Mill. Tel. 156. Erie, B. R. & P., and W. N. Y. & P. sidings.

Bradford Hardwood Lumber Co., Lewis Emery, Jr., president; J. B. Etherington, vice president; B. M. Bailey, secretary, treasurer and manager. Manufacturers of woven wire mattress frames and cot frames. Dimension stock of all descriptions from hardwood lumber. Control own timber lands and operate band saw mill at Bradford, capacity, 30,000 feet per day; also at Lewis Run, capacity, 30,000 feet per day. Average number people employed 200. Principal office and factory at Bradford, Pa. Cor. Jackson ave. and Mill. Tel. 156. Erie, B. R. & P., and W. N. Y. & P. sidings.

Union Dish Company, Limited, Dr. A. M. Straight, president; C. S. Olmstead, treasurer; S. A. Holbrook, secretary and manager. Manufacturers of wood tooth-picks, butchers' skewers, wood butter dishes and baskets. Capacity, $100,000 per year. Employing 75 people. Office and works in Sixth ward, East Bradford.

Standard Wood Company, James W. Blaisdell, president; W. F. Blaisdell, vice president; George T. Whyte, secretary and treasurer; P. C. Blaisdell, general manager at Bradford. Manufacturers of and wholesale dealers in kiln-dried bundle wood. Principal office, 120-122 Liberty street, near York. Controlling 13 factories. Capacity, Bradford works, 100,000 bundles per day. employing 160 people. Works, foot Blaisdell ave. Tel. 204.

Bradford City Glass Bottle Works, A. De Golier and J. H. Smart, proprs. Manufacturers of flint green flasks, soda and beer bottles. Capacity one continuos tank, seven rings, or about 120 gross per day. Employing 60 people. Office and factory on Erie railroad, near foot of Sherman. Tel. 134.

Victor Dish Company, Alex. Watson, manager. Manufacturers of wooden butter dishes. Office and works, 81 Hilton. Tel. 233.

Watson & Meachem (Alex. Watson and William Meachem), Manufacturers of rig irons, reels and tanks. Office and works, 81 Hilton. Tel. 233.

R. Hannahs, Manufactures tinware of all kinds. Wholesale and retail dealer. 393 East Main.

Charles J. Tremaine, Manufacturer of and dealer in the Sectional Fuel Gas Burners for cook stoves. Office 17 Mechanic.

National Brick Company (Corporation), L. E. Hamsher, general manager; W. R. Weaver, secretary and treasurer. Manufacturers of standard and ornamental fine red pressed brick Sidewalk brick a specialty. Works located at Lewis Run, on B., R. & P. and Erie railroads. General offices, 41 Main. Tel. 120.

The Triumph Inhaler Company, Dr. C. P. Alling, propr. Manufactures Dr. Alling's Triumph Inhaler and Dr. Alling's Amara, a stomach and nerve tonic. 9-11-13 Moore block, over 68 Main.

MARBLE WORKS.

Allen & Hodges (H. E. Allen, J. Hodges). Granite and Marble works. Monuments, table tops, counters, mantels. 9 Chestnut.

Foley Bros. (Peter C., John P.), P. J. Heysel, manager. Granite and Marble Monumental works. Wood and slate mantels. Grates and tile. Office and Works, opp. Oak Hill cemetery, 187 East Main.

MASQUERADE COSTUMER.

Miss E. Keenan, Over 3 Webster.

MEATS AND PROVISIONS.

The G. H. Hammond Co., J. A. Winsor, manager. Wholesale dealers in Chicago dressed beef and provisions. 37-39 Webster. Tel. 228.

Swift & Co., W. B. Morrison, manager. Wholesale dealers in Swift's choice dressed beef, Cor. Webster and Elm. Tel. 250.

MEAT MARKETS.

J. Kilgore, Fresh and smoked meats. Poultry, lard, butter, eggs, etc. 89 Main. Tel. 211.

Excelsior Meat Market, Mrs. C. Spangler, propr., George W. Spangler, manager. Fresh and salt meats. Poultry and oysters in season. 80 Main. Tel. 205.

William H. Bloom, Fresh meats, poultry and oysters. Also bread, pies and cakes. Cor. Elm and Chestnut. Tel. 241-B.

G. A. Williams, Fresh and salt meats, 158 Main.

A. T. Herrington, Wholesale and retail dealer in fresh, salt and pickled meats. Poultry and game. 77 Mechanic. Tel 48.

A. J. Hempstead, Fresh and salt meats. Oysters, poultry and game in season. 63 Mechanic.

W. C. Davis, Fresh and salt meats. Poultry and oysters in season. 20 Congress. Tel. 254.

W. A. Winsor, Fresh, smoked and salt meats. Oysters and poultry. 91 Washington, Cor. Pearl.

J. F. Hubbard & Son (La Vern), Dealers in meats of all kinds. Home-made sausages a specialty. 40 Davis. Tel. 240.

James McGraw, Fresh and salt meats and home-made sausages. Fish and oysters. 47 Pearl, cor. School. Tel. 207-F.

Model Market, Jacob Heckel, proprietor. Fresh, salt and smoked meats. Poultry and oysters in season. Home-made sauerkraut. 62 Corydon. Tel. 218.

Brooklin Market, R. E. McIntyre, proprietor. Dealer in fresh, salt and smoked meats. Oysters, poultry and game in season. 59 Barbour. Tel. 207.

Story & Co., Fresh and salt meats. Home-dressed poultry and oysters in season. 93 Washington.

D. P. Andres, Fresh and salt meats. 407 East Main.

M. Thessen, Fresh and salt meats. Poultry and oysters in season. 400 East Main.

L. Bailey, Fresh and salt meats. Poultry and oysters. 138 So. Mechanic. Tel. 242.

M. J. Foster, Fresh and salt meats. Poultry and oysters. Fruits and vegetables. 40 Miller.

M. Garfinkle, Fresh and salt meats. Poultry and oysters. 73 Washington.

Ungemach & Co., George Ungemach, manager. Fresh and salt meats. 67 Congress.

L. M. Wynkoop, Fresh and smoked meats, 4-6 Brennan.

Carr Bros. (F. B. & A.), Fresh and salt meats, poultry, etc. 177 E. Main.

W. H. Toy, Meat dealer, 7 Florence.

Wolf Cohn, Jewish meat market, 16 Congress.

SHOES FOR COMFORT.

LOUIS SENDKER,

Anatomical Shoe Maker and Surgeon Chiropodist,

ALSO DEALER IN

BOOTS AND SHOES,

70 Main Street and 7 Pine Street.

SENDKER'S ANATOMICAL SHOE.

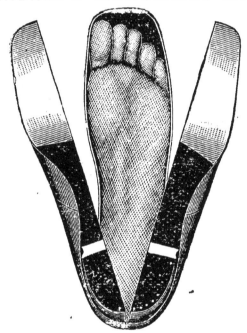

Lasts made to fit the feet and reserved for customers. Measures once taken, always reserved. Goods sent to any part of the country.

.A Full Line of Men's and Boys' Shoes
ALWAYS ON HAND AT POPULAR PRICES.

The Only First Class Custom Shop in the Cit
Repairing Neatly Done at Reasonable Prices.

AUGUSTUS MILLER.   FRED A. MILLER.

A. MILLER & SON,

LUMBER
SHINGLES

SASH, DOORS, GLASS AND WEIGHTS,

Turned Work a Specialty.
Long Distance Telephone.

Office, No. 86 Kennedy Street.
Sheds and Yard in Rear.

BRADFORD,   **PENN'A.**

EUGENE ELLISON,
Teacher of Violin

Nothing but the Best Methods Used.
STUDIO—161 JACKSON AVENUE,

G. R. MABB,
Lock and Gunsmith.

Manufacturer of Rubber and Steel Stamps,
Corporation and Lodge Seals, Stencils, Brass
and German Silver Checks, Badges, etc.

UMBRELLAS REPAIRED AND RE-COVERED.
BICYCLE REPAIRING.

7 Congress Street,   -   -   Bradford, Pa.

MERCHANT TAILORS.

C. N. Pfohl, Importing tailor, 55 Main.

H. Wollman, Ladies' tailor, over 57 Main.

White, the Tailor (Wm. H. White), over 53 Main.

Flynn & Friedman (J. E. Flynn, S. J. Friedman), 103 Main.

Joseph Tronstein, 109 Main.

T. F. O'Day, Tailor and cutter, over 38 Main.

Patrick Crowley, General tailoring business. Room 2, over 102 Main.

George Habernigg, 16 Chambers.

John Weiss, Merchant tailor and gents' furnishing goods, 58 Main.

H. L. McCoy, 90 Main.

Sterling Custom Tailoring Co. F. Freerkson), proprietor. Popular priced tailor. Twelve tailors constantly employed. 11 Main.

N. Wise, Merchant tailor. 9 Congress.

H. M. Wohlford & Co. (Successors to C. E. Horton & Co.), Ladies' and gents' tailors. Rooms 1-2-3, Producers Exchange. Public square.

Olaf Johnson, 12 Chambers.

MILK DEPOTS.

G. N. Story, Milk and cream, 95 Washington.

Rickards & Walruth (Richard I. Rickards, Gilbert N. Walruth.) Milk and cream. Also butter, eggs and vegetables. Cor. Chestnut and Elm.

John Healy, Milk and cream, 18 Congress.

J. F. Hubbard & Son, Milk and cream. 40 Davis. Tel. 240.

Rumsey's Creamery, H. Rumsey, propr. Milk and cream. 65 Congress. Tel. 139-B. Branch depot at 37 Kennedy. Tel 253-B.

Medberry & London, 163 Main.

MILLINERS.

Robert B. Johnston, Art millinery and ladies' fine furnishings. 53 Main. (See dry goods.)

Mrs. M. Schermerhorn, Millinery and fancy goods. 399 East Main.

Mrs. T. D. Nash, Millinery, ribbons, velvets, laces, tips, feathers, etc. 76 Mechanic.

Mrs. A. M. Selden, Ladies' and children's millinery. 52 Mechanic.

Mrs. P. F. Schoonover, Millinery, over 388 East Main.

Miss L. B. McKay, Fine millinery. 32 Main. Cor. Congress.

The Bazar, Millinery. [See dry goods.]

Racket Store, Millinery. 6-8-10-12 Kennedy.

The Fair, Millinery. 22 Main. [See dry goods.]

The French Millinery Parlors, Over 93 Main.

Miss E. Keenan, Millinery, over 3, Webster.

MINING COMPANIES.

Inca Mining Company, C. P. Collins, president; W. R. Weaver, secretary and treasurer. Office, 8 Exchange Lyceum. 35 Main.

Adit=Dew Drop Mining Company, Harry N. Richmond, repre-sentative. Office, over 34-36 Main.

MUSIC DEALERS.

W. L. Gilson, Agent for Keller Bros.' pianos. Also piano tuner. 84 High.

Jacob Sheasley, Pianos, organs, sewing machines, Mu-sical merchandise of all kinds. 99 Main. Tel. 247-B.

M. H. Miller, Musical instruments and jewelry. 69 Me-chanic.

C. E. Harrington, Pianos and organs, 21 Congress.

Mrs. S. E. Morrison, Pianos and organs, 33 Foreman.

B. F. Rothstein, New and second-hand musical instruments and merchandise. 54 Main, Opera House block.

G. A. Fry, Pianos, organs. sewing machines, and all kinds of musical merchandise. New and socond-hand pianos to rent. 15 Kennedy.

MUSICAL INSTRUMENTS—MAKERS AND REPAIRERS.

E. J. Reed, Violin maker and repairer. All string instru-ments repaired. 87 Washington.

M. L. Akerly, Musical instruments of all kinds repaired. 22 Patent alley.

MUSICAL ORGANIZATIONS.

Jamison's Orchestra, J. W. Jamison, manager. Record: Eighteen years at the Wagoner Opera House. Ten consecutive seasons at the Kent House, Lakewood, Chautauqua Lake. Four seasons en route in con-cert. Headquarters at Option House. Tel. 263.

Evincible Band and Orchestra. M. L. Akerly, manager. 22 Patent alley.

Ronan's Orchestra. E. J. Ponan, manager: R. M. Klingen-smith, leader. Ten professional musicians. Concert and dance music a specialty. Headquarters Mansion House.

Sixteenth Regiment Band, Joseph Tronstein, president; M. G. Raub, secretary; R. W. Murray, treasurer; Paul Charles, leader. Headquarters at Armory.

O. F. Spencer Band, E. A. Stillwagon, president: C. V, Cottrell, business manager; Chauncey Shysman. secretary; Wm. Dugan, leader. Headquarters K. O. T. M. hall, East Main.

NEWSDEALERS.

C. V. Cottrell, 95 Main.

Brennan & Davis, 21 Main.

W. L. Field, 110 Main.

John C. Calhoun & Son, 412 East Main. Tel. connection.

J. E. Abbott, Agent for Saturday Globe (Utica, N. Y.) 120 Washington. Tel. 149-K.

John Tierney, Agent for Buffalo Courier-Record, News and Times. 73 Summer.

NEWSPAPERS.

The Bradford Era, Published every morning, except Sunday, by the Era Publishing company, at 15-19 Exchange Place. Republican. P. C. Boyle, manager; H. J. Bryan, business manager: D. A. Dennison, editor; W. F. Potter. city editor. Tel. 184.

The Bradford Weekly Era, Published every Thursday at 15-19 Exchange Place by the Era Publishing company. P. C. Boyle, manager.

The Bradford Daily Record, Published every afternoon, except Sunday, by the Record company. at 11 Exchange Place. Republican. R. E. Whiteley, editor and manager. Tel. 163.

The Bradford Evening Star, Published every afternoon, except Sunday, by the Star Publishing company, at 8 Public Square. Republican. R. B. Stone. president; Horace G. James. business manager. Tel. 291.

The Weekly Star-Mail, Published every Friday by the Star Publishing company at 8 Public Square.

Bradford Sunday Herald, Published every Saturday and Sunday morning at 134 South Mechanic. Independent, not neutral. W. L. Cooper, editor and publisher. Tel. 151.

The Bradford Sunday Post, Published every Sunday morning at rear 61 Main, upstairs. Republican. George O. Slone, manager; J. F. Robinson, city editor. Tel. 199.

OIL BUYERS.

Joseph Seep Purchasing Agency, J. B. Skelly, agent. 69-71 Main. Tel. 215.

Emery Pipe Line, J. L. Johnson, agent. 41 Main. Tel. 120

The Tide-Water Pipe Line Company, Ltd., Henry Byrom, agent. 118-120 Mechanic, St. James block. Tel. 159.

OIL CARRIERS.

W. W. Laraway, Retail dealer in refined oils, 1 Matteson place.

M. H. Murphy, Dealer in refined oils, 19 Boylston.

OIL COMPANIES.

Devonian Oil Co., C. P. Collins, president: J. R. Leonard, treasurer: J. H. Evans, secretary. Offices 7-9-10 Exchange Lyceum, 35 Main. Tel. 295.

Mallory & Rathbone, (L. E. Mallory, Chas. H. Rathbone) Office 5 Exchange Lyceum, 35 Main. Tel. 166.

Mallory & Matson Oil Co. (L. E. Mallory, Myron Matson) Office 5 Exchange Lyceum, 35 Main. Tel. 166.

Northern Oil Co., T. N. Barnsdall, president; Wm. Barnsdall, Jr.. vice president; E. P. Whitcomb, secretary and treasurer. Office 22 Congress, Tel. 287.

Hydro-Carbon Oil Co., Ltd., Fred W. Winger, president; A. J. Edgett, vice president; G. E. Benninghoff, treasurer: S. A. Holbrook, secretary. Office 7, Dikeman block. 34 Main. Tel. 140-B.

Hazelwood Oil Co., H. G. Barcroft, superintendent. Office in Pompelon hall, Public Square. Tel 23.

South Penn Oil Co., (Midland division), J. C. McKinney, general manager. Office 69-71 Main. Tel. 123.

Test Oil Company, Wm. H. Johnson, president: E. T. Johnson. vice president: Walter H. Johnson, secretary and treasurer. Office, 157 Mechanic.

Parm Oil Company, W. L. Curtis. manager, 8 Producers' Exchange.

Superior Oil Company, C. P. Collins. president; J. H. Hardison. vice president; Harry Heasley, secretary; J. R. Leonard. treasurer. 10 Lyceum. Tel. 295.

Emery Oil Company (Partnership), L. Emery, Jr., W. R. Weaver, L. E. Hamsher. L. E. Hamsher, general manager: W. R. Weaver, treasurer. 41 Main. Tel. 120.

Matson Oil Company (Partnership), M. Matson, Emery Oil company and Devonian Oil company L. E. Hamsher, superintendent; W. R. Weaver. treasurer. 41 Main. Tel. 120.

Quintuple Oil Company (Partnership). Emery Oil company, South Penn Oil company and S. A. Wheeler. L. E. Hamsher. superintendent: W. R. Weaver, treasurer. 41 Main Tel. 120.

Caldwell, Hamsher & Co. (Partnership), R. Caldwell, L. E. Hamsher. L. Emery. Jr. R. Caldwell. manager. 41 Main. Tel. 120.

Hamsher, Weaver & Co. (Partnership). L. E. Hamsher, W. R. Weaver, L. Emery, Jr. L. E. Hamsher, superintendent, 41 Main. Tel. 120.

Phœnix Oil Company, F. D. Wood. treas. 19 Main. Tel. 273.

McCrum Oil Company, John McCrum. Kenton Saulnier, Frank Glaeser, George C. Fagnan. John McCrum, secretary and treasurer: Frank Glaeser, general manager. Office over 94 Main.

Lynx Oil and Gas Company, James McManus, J. W. Matthews, J. L. Moss, H. C. Heffner, F. G. Howe. W. J. McDonell, J. M. Coleman, Bradford, Pa.

Great Foam Oil Company, G. E. Benninghoff, chairman; C. A. Ralph, secretary and treasurer; 30½ Main.

OIL INSPECTOR.

Charles A. Filkins. State Oil Inspector, 63 Kennedy.

OIL PRODUCERS.

Coleman, Penny & Boyne (E. W. Coleman, William J. Penny, E. A. Boyne). 8 Produces' Exchange, Public Square.

C. B. Whitehead, 155 Jackson ave. Tel. 145-F.

Ralph Bros. (I. C , J. H.. S. E.), 4 Berry & Melvin block, 18 Main.

L. B. Lockard, Whitney Place.

P. H. Davitt, 53 Mechanic. Tel. 118.

J. T. Jones, 24 Congress. Tel. 292.

T. N. Barnsdall, 22 Congress. Tel 287.

William Barnsdall, Jr., 22 Congress. Tel. 287.

E. P. Whitcomb, 22 Congress. Tel. 287.

A. J. Edgett, 1 Congress. Tel. 125.

Bisett Bros., (E. W.. J. J., C. F. and W.) 19 Webster. Tel. 214.

S. G. Coffin, 12 Barbour. Tel. 136.

T. P. Thompson, 5 Producers' Exchange, Public Square.

C. P. Collins, 6 Exchange Lyceum, 35 Main. Tel. 295.

R. J. Straight, over 67 Main. Tel. 35.

L. E. Mallory, 5 Exchange Lyceum, 35 Main. Tel.: Office, 166. Residence, 138.

Charles H. Rathbone, 5 Exchange Lyceum, 35 Main. Tel. 166,

Myron Matson, 41 Main. Tel. 120.

Boggs, Rosenberg & Co. (O. P. Boggs, J. Rosenberg, W. L. Curtis), 8 Producers' Exchange, Public Square.

Jabez Rogerson, 189 Congress.

W. D. Burdick, Riddell House. Tel. 262.

William Hanley, 18 Jackson ave.

Caldwell, Hamsher & Co. (R. Caldwell, L. E. Hamsher, L Emery, Jr.), 41 Main. Tel. 120.

J. C. Greenewald, 124 Main.

Lewis E. Hamsher, 41 Main. Tel. 120.

W. R. Weaver, 41 Main. Tel. 120.

Lewis Emery, Jr., 41 Main. Tel. 120.

S. P. Kennedy, 67 Main.

T. H. Kennedy, 67 Main.

T. J. Melvin, 3 Berry & Melvin block, 18 Main. Tel. 192.

A. J. McKeown, 60 Kennedy. Tel. 154.

C. S. Whitney, 5 St. James Place. Tel. 128.

J. D. Wolf, 20 Producers' Exchange, Public Square.

A. L. Wyman, 124 Main. Tel. 145-B.

Willis M. Kincaid, 10 Exchange Lyceum, 35 Main. Tel. 295.
Kuno Kuhn, Room 21, Imperial Hotel.
C. W. Lockard, 26 Elm.
Robert Long, 65 Jackson ave.
John H Markham, 99 Congress,
Eugene McElwaine. 215 Mechanic.
James B. Steele. 27 Jefferson.
A. B. Walker, 95 Kennedy.
W. P. Thompson, 49 Kennedy.
Thomas E. McCray, 107 Kennedy.
F. E. Van Wormer, 51 Amm.
J. H. Van Wormer, 51 Amm.
George Woodard, 41 Boylston.
George Woodard, Jr., 41 Boylston.
E. W. Cooper. 27 Boylston.
John Fitzgibbon, 69 Boylston.
F. A. Moore, 56 Boylston.
Robert Roy, 85 Boylston.
John S. Wilson, 58 Pleasant.
Samuel R. Rhodes, 105 Centre.
Clinton G. Boyd, 103 School.
George H. Potter, 82 School. Tel. 50.
Charles O'Donnell, 40 Walker ave.
Charles De Hart, 12 Jackson ave.
David F. Connolly, 14 Foreman.
Chas. A. Spreeter, 2 Foreman.
H. W. Ford, 9 Petrolia.
Henry W. Tracy. 11 Petrolia.
Allan Cochran, 14 Sanford.
James Furman, 24 Sanford.
C. C. Melvin, 81 Corydon.
Thomas Scroxton, 129 Corydon.
W. H. Emery, Corydon extension.
John Healey, 151 Corydon.
Frank S. Palmer, Corydon extension.
Lesser H. Cohn, 86 Corydon.
C. G. Urquhart, 112 Main.
William M. Urquhart, 118 Main.
W. C. Kennedy, 67 Main.
Thomas McDonell, 112 Main.
O. F. Schonblom, 67 Main. Tel. 131.
J. S. Barlow, 32 Boylston.
John J. Friedley, third floor, Lyceum, 35 Main. Tel. 59.
A. C. Hawkins, Lyceum, 35 Main. Tel. 182.
F. W. Davis, 52 Jackson ave. Tel. 121-B.

C. N. Owens, 132 Congress.
A. F. Bannon, 133 Congress.
C. P. Byron, 111 Congress.
George Dana, 108 Congress.
James R. Goldsboro, 91 Congress.
J. E. Haskell, 40 Congress.
J. K. Merriam, 41 Congress.
Morris Shear, 113 Congress.
John W. Siggins, 105 Congress.
C. H. Cutting, 325 South Mechanic.
Stella M Neal, 194 South Mechanic.
J. R. Pomeroy, 156 South Mechanic.
W. J. McVay, 2 Washington.
William Chambers, 11 Chautauqua.
A. T. Herrick, 18 Bushnell.
George S. Van Vechten, 141 Davis.
J. A. Connolly, 2 Bishop.
Louis H. Cohn, 45 Kennedy.
F. T. Davis, 48 Kennedy.
Samuel A. Taft, 43 Amm.
E. M. Wheeler, 60 East Main.
A. D Van Norman, 357 East Main.
A. B. Clark, 363 East Main.
J. P. Eaton, 73 East Main.
John Q. Field, 330 East Main.
A. V. Field, 353 East Main.
C. H. Foster, 222 East Main.
W. Harris, 359 East Main.
Homer C. Jones, 357 East Main.
John K. Mitchell, 406 East Main.
Willis N. Schoonover. 236 East Main.
A. Anderson, 96 Jackson ave.
John Barry, 139 Jackson ave.
Samuel W. McMurray, 76 Jackson ave.
George W. Crooks, 56 Cornen.
A. W. Wheeler, 175 Kendall ave.
Thomas Nolan, East end Kendall ave.
James W. Gormerley, 199 Kendall ave.
Charles A. Martin, 48 Kendall ave.
Charles B. Stoddard, 20 Sanford.
Bernard Gunn, 16 Jerome ave.
N. Wells, cor. Oxford and Rockland aves.
John W. McCray, 28 Jefferson.
George R. Griffin, 1 Thompson ave.
Andrew Gordnier, 63 High.

Peter Hannan, High extension.

Wm. W. Cartmell, 11 Chamberlain ave.

W. P. Hyde, 12 Kingsbury ave.

James B. Pierson, 18 Hill.

John H. Logan, 97 Summer.

John McGillis, over 122 Main.

Geo. R. Brown, Room 2, over 112 Main.

Wm. J. McDonell, Room 2, over 105 Main.

J. N. Coleman, Room 2, over 105 Main.

Frank J. Newton, Room 2, over 105 Main.

C. H. Johnston, Room 2, over 105 Main.

T. A. Shanley, Room 2, over 105 Main.

Timothy Murphy, Room 16, over 86 Main.

Jacob West, Room 7. over 88 Main.

J. M. Tait, 110 Corydon.

Timothy Coughlin, 5 Terrace.

F. M. Jordan. over 67 Congress.

F. M. Johnston, 134 Congress.

John W. Vantine, 138 Congress.

Patrick Manrow, 199 Congress.

Harlow B. Pike, 271 South Mechanic.

E. L. Smedley, 222 South Mechanic.

Thomas D. Smedley, 222 South Mechanic.

Wm. H. Duncan, 10 Potter.

Alfred E. Parker, 3 Potter.

Sherman B. Dunham, 157 South Mechanic.

Norman Parker, 29 William.

Thomas Piper, 93 Summer.

George C. Fagnan, 117 Main.   Tel. 175.

Kenton Saulnier, over 94 Main.

John McCrum, over 94 Main.

Frank Glaeser over 94 Main.

H. H North, over 110 Mechanic.

OIL WELL SUPPLIES.

The National Supply Company, Joseph L. Wolcott. president; Henry M. Wilson, first vice president; William Hardee, second vice president; H. W. Bishop, third vice president; W. C. Hillman, general manager; Sibbet McCrum, treasurer; E. B. King, assistant treasurer; J. H. Barr, secretary.   Capital, $1,000,000.   C. A. Ralph, manager Bradford store.   Dealers in oil well supplies, tubing, casing, line, steam and drive pipe. Engines, boilers and cordage.   Shop on Elm, cor. Erie railroad.   Tel. 127-B.   Store, 30½ Main.   Tel. 127.

L. Emery, Jr., & Co., Oil well supplies, tubing, casing and pipe. 43-45 Main. Tel. 274. (See Hardware).

Bovaird & Seyfang Manufacturing Company, 30 Davis. Tel. 164. (See Iron, Brass and Steel Works).

Tuna Iron Works, 61-63 Elm. Tel. 282. (See Iron, Brass and Steel Works).

Kimball & McClellan (C. C. Kimball, S. M. McClellan), Dealers in second-hand oil well supplies. Rear 115 Main.

Bovaird & Co. (J. H. Bovaird, W. J. Bovaird, A. B. Booth), D. Bovaird, manager. Machine and boiler shop. Boilers, engines, pipe, tubing, rods, casing, rig irons, tanks and oil well supplies. Office and shops, 143 Main. Tel. 110.

Oil Well Supply Company, Store, 94 Main, cor. Webster. Tel. 115 (See Iron, Brass and Steel Works).

Bayne, Wilson & Pratt, W. M. Kincaid, manager. Boilers and engines, tubing and casing, line, steam and drive pipe. Office, Room 10, Exchange Lyceum. 35 Main. Tel. 295.

Lever Engine Co., C. L. Wheeler, secretary and treasurer. Manufacturers of patented lever engines. Office 144 South Mechanic.

OIL WORKS AND REFINERIES.

Emery Manufacturing Company, Lewis Emery, Jr., proprietor and manager. Producers, refiners and transporters of petroleum and its products. Manufacturers of high grade refined oil, mineral lubricating oils, paraffine, waxes, benzine, naphtha, gasolene, etc. Employing 50 people. Works cover 6½ acres. Erie, B., R. & P. and W. N. Y. & P. sidings. Principal office, 41 Main. Tel. 120. Works, foot Hilton street on B., R. & P. railroad. Tel. 37.

Journal Oil Company, H. J. Haggerty, proprietor; J. Haggerty, manager. Manufacturers of cylinder and machine oils, crank pin grease, wagon grease and Haggerty's cooling compound. Office and works opposite Erie freight depot. Tel. 107-F.

Orient Refining Company, R. J. Hoffman, proprietor and manager. Works at East Bradford on B., R. & P. railroad. Office, 5 Potter,

Hoffman Lubricating Oil Company, R. J. Hoffman, proprietor. Works at East Bradford on B., R. & P. railroad. Office, 5 Potter,

Penn Lubricating Oil Company, R. J. Hoffman, propr. Works at East Bradford on B., R. & P. railroad. Office, 5 Potter.

Kendall Refining Co., N. B. Barnsdall, propr. Refiners of petroleum. Manufacturers of lubricating oils, cyclinder oils and machine oils, naphtha, etc. Office and works on B. R. & P. Railroad, near Kendall ave.

W. W. Green, Manufacturer of harness oil stock. Works on Clark farm, on line of O. R. C. & B. St. Ry.

Hamilton Lubricating Oil Company, E. A. Hamilton, propr. Manufacturers of high grade valve and engine oils, cup and axle grease, bicycle and sewing machine oils. Office 21 Chestnut. Works near B. B. & K. trestle.

PAINTERS AND PAPER HANGERS.

John Canty, 20 Patent alley or 107 Pleasant.

Charles Ingersoll, 42 Main.

F. G. Wilbur, Room 3, Moore block, 88 Main.

W. A. O'Day, Sign painter, 31 Kennedy.

V. D. Godfrey, House and sign painter. Over 9 Pine.

C. J. Barr, Paper hanging and painting. 98 Washington. Up stairs.

W. M. Holmes, Painter and paper hanger. 56½ East Main.

Samuel A. Mooney, House and sign painter and paper hanger. 23 Davis.

Sandborn & Son (S. A., Fred), Contractors House painting and paper hanging. 40 school.

George Harnden, Sign painting. Over 30 Main.

J. H. Whitney, House painter and grainer. Over 30 Main.

T. C. Hunter, House painter. Over 30 Main.

James Franklin, House painter and grainer, 5 Walker Place.

PAWN BROKERS.

B. F. Rothstein, Licensed pawn broker. Dealer in watches, clocks, jewelry, silverware. 54 Main, Opera House block. (See jewelry.)

Rothstein & Lippman Bros., 7 Main.

PATENT ATTORNEYS.

Ben R. Hagar, Patent attorney and draftsman. Room 1, over 38 Main.

H. H. North, Patent attorney. Office, 1-2 Sheehy block, 110 Mechanic.

PENSION ATTORNEYS.

E. R. Sherman, Over 30 Main.

M. G. Cline, Over 81 Mechanic.

PICTURE FRAMES.

Otto Koch, Picture frames and mouldings, 139-141 South Mechanic. Tel. 129.

F. E. Kathan, Picture framing. Complete line of mouldings. 136 South Mechanic.

Chappell's Art Store, Picture frames and art goods. 12 Boylston.

PIPE LINES.

United States Pipe Line Company, Lewis Emery, Jr., president; Eugene Liebel, secretary; E. H. Jennings, treasurer. 2-3-4 Exchange Lyceum, 35 Main. Tel. 166.

The Tide-Water Pipe Line Company, Ltd., S. Q. Brown, chairman; R. E. Hopkins, secretary; J. H. Cuthbert, treasurer; S. Q. Brown, R. D. Benson, R. E. Hopkins, J.

H. Cuthbert, H. C. Fahnestock, managers: J. G. Benton. general superintendent; J. H. Dickson, superintendent main lines; **A. W. Golden**, superintendent local lines; J. E. Golden, superintendent telegraph; W. S. Batchelder, oil purchasing agent. Principal office at Titusville. Henry Byrom, agent at Bradford. Offices 118-120 Mechanic, St. James block. Tel. 159.

National Transit Company, John O'Brien, superintendent; E. R. Shepard, agent. Office 69-71 Main. Tel. 215.

PHOTOGRAPHERS.

Charles F. Schwab, Platino finish a specialty, 59 Main.

Frank Robbins, Photographer and dealer in kodaks and phonographs. Over 83 Main.

Mrs. West's Studio, Mrs. M. M. West, propr. Ladies' and children's work a specialty. Only lady photographer in the city. Over 14 Congress.

Hartford Photo Company, F. W. Hotchkiss, prop. General photo work. 3 Chestnut.

East End Photographer, Horace Kern, propr, 429 East Main, opp. American House.

PHYSICIANS AND SURGEONS.

Dr. C. D. Buss, Eye, ear and throat, specialist. Office practice. Over 9 Main.

Drs. Benninghoff & Stewart (George E. Benninghoff, James B. Stewart). Dr. Benninghoff's office hours, 1:30 to 3:30 and 7 to 8 p. m. Dr. Stewart's office hours, 10 to 12 a. m., 3:30 to 5:30 and 7 to 8 p. m. Over 9 Main. Tel. 102.

Dr. James Johnston, Office hours, 1 to 4 and 6 to 8 p. m. Over 13 Main. Tel. 278-B.

Dr. H. J. Nichols, Office hours, 1 to 3 and 7 to 8 p. m. Davis block, over 21 Main. Tel. 49-B.

Dr. Adelaide M. Griffin, Eye, ear and throat specialist and general practice. Office hours, 10 to 12 a. m., 2 to 5 p. m. Over 55 Main.

Dr. C. S. Hubbard, Office hours, 11 to 12 a. m., 3 to 4 and 7 to 8 p. m. Over 61 Main.

Dr. Emily A. Corbin, Diseases of women a specialty. Office hours, 10 to 12 a. m. and 3 to 6 p. m. Over 83 Main.

Dr. H. A. Canfield, Office hours, 9 to 12 a. m.. 2 to 5 p. m. Over 95 Main. Tel. office, 148; residence, 139.

Dr. F. C. Cluxton, Office hours, 9 to 12, 2 to 5 and 7 to 8. Over 111 Main.

Dr. J. J. Cannan,Office hours. 1 to 4 and 7 to 10. Over 117 Main. Tel. 175.

Dr. S. B. Dorn, Office hours, 1 to 4 p. m. Room 10, El oskey block. Over 24 Main. Tel. 82.

Dr. A. Grace White, Office hours. 8 to 10 a, m.. 2 to 5 p. m. Over 83 Main. Tel. office, 240-B; residence, 153.

Drs. Straight & Walker (A. M. Straight, J. C. Walker). Dr. Straight's office hours, 7:30 to 8:30 a. m. and 2 to 4 p. m. Dr. Walker's office hours, 9 to 10 a. m.. 3 to 4 and 7:30 to 8:30 p. m. Over 34 Main, Dikeman block. Tel. 140-F.

Dr. W. J. Russell, Office hours, 2 to 4 and 7 to 8 p. m. Over 34 Main, Dikeman block. Tel. office, 140-B; residence, 18.

Dr. F. W. Winger, Office hours 2 to 4 and 7 to 8 p. m. Over 34 Main. Dikeman block. Tel: office 140-B, res. 42.

Dr. C. P. Alling, Diseases of women and orificial surgery a specialty. Offices, rooms 9-11-13. Moore building. 88 Main. Tel. 71.

Dr. M. A. Todd, Office hours 9 to 10 a. m., 2 to 4 and 7 to 9 p. m. Over 92 Main. Tel. at res. 2.

Dr. H. P. Holt, Eye, ear and electricity a specialty. Office hours 9 to 12 a. m.. 2 to 5 and 7 to 8 p. m. Rooms 2-3, Newell building. 98 Main.

Dr. S. H. Haines, Office hours until 9 a. m., 12 to 3 and 7 to 9 p. m. 404 East Main. Tel. 116-F.

Dr. D. E. Ash, Office hours 1 to 3 p. m. 414 East Main. Tel. at res. 272-K.

Dr. J. W. King, Office hours 8:30 to 10 a. m.. 1 to 4 and 7 to 8:30 p. m. Over 13 Main. Tel. 278-B.

Dr. G. W. Rae, Office hours, 10 to 12 a. m., 2 to 4 p. m. Over 78 Mechanic.

Dr. E. A. Van Scoy, Office hours, 8 to 9 a. m., 2 to 4 and 7 to 8 p. m. 101 Corydon. Tel. 95.

Dr. E. Grewer, All chronic and nervous diseases a specialty. Office hours, 9 to 12 a. m., 2 to 5 and 7 to 9 p. m. Rooms 4-5-6 Eloskey building, 24 Main Over Bazar.

Dr. W. R. Gibson, Office hours. 9 a. m., 1 to 4 and 7 to 8:30 p. m. Tel. 278-B. Over 15 Main.

Dr. H. S. Baker, Office and residence, 48 Bennett Brook road.

Dr. A. H. Southwick, 34 Main. Tel. 140.

Dr. H. H. Stearns, Office hours, 2 to 4 p. m. Over 34 Main. Tel 140-F.

Dr. J. E. Hayes, Offices, 4-5 Eloskey building. 24 Main.

PLUMBERS.

Lewis & Co. (T. F. and E. W. Lewis), General plumbers. Hot water, steam and gas fitting. 16 Pine. Tel. 103.

Bradford Plumbing and Heating Company, C. H. Daniels, manager; J. Daniels, treasurer. Sanitary plumbing and gas fitting. Hot water heating. 15 Congress.

A. D. Burns, Plumbing, steam and hot water heating and gas fitting. 14 Public Square. Tel. 238.

H. C. Carr, Plumbing, steam and gas fitting, etc. 18 Kennedy. Tel. 259-B.

Pennsylvania Plumbing and Heating Company (T. J. Butler, G. H. Drake), plumbing, steam and hot water heating and gas fitting. Plumbing supplies of all kinds. 15 Davis.

A. T. Ralph, Plumbing and gas fitting and tinsmith. 75 Washington.

O. E. David, 11 Chestnut.

PRINTERS AND BOOKBINDERS.

B. Gilson, Bookbinding exclusively. Room 22 Exchange Lyceum. 35 Main.

D. W. Lerch, Book and job printing of all kinds. Bookbinding. Rear 61 Main. ·

James W. Leasure, General job printing and bookbinding. 17 Main. Tel. 179.

Star Publishing Company, Job printing. 8 Public Square. Tel. 291.

Slone & Slone (R. H. and G. O.), General job printers and manufacturers of rubber stamps. 8 Chestnut.

PRODUCE AND COMMISSION.

McEvoy Bros. (John E. McEvoy), Wholesale commission house. 84 Main. Tel. 281.

Beal, Simons & Co. (J. W. Beal, W. H Simons, J. A. Green), Wholesale produce and commission merchants. 131 Main. Tel 172.

Sillesky & Scott (John M. Sillesky, Wm. C. Scott), Wholesale dealers in produce and fruit. 13 Webster. Tel. 106-F.

Washington Jewell, Wholesale and retail dealer in produce and fruit. 44 Corydon.

PROVISIONS.

Rickards & Walruth, Butter, eggs and vegetables. Cor. Chestnut and Elm.

John Johnson, Butter, eggs, cheese, hams, etc. 16 Congress.

J. A. Butterfield, 65 Mechanic.

RAILROAD COMPANIES.

Buffalo, Rochester & Pittsburg Railroad Company, J. T. Gardner, superintendent Pittsburg division; W. W. Brogan, chief train dispatcher; A. J. Johnson, superintendent Buffalo division; E. I. Blair, chief train dispatcher; J. C. McCray, special agent; L. B. McIntyre, freight and passenger agent. Offices at depot. Tel. 243.

Erie Railroad, C. V. Merrick, superintendent Bradford division; F. A. Fralic, chief clerk; F. J. Goodfellow, division freight agent; F. M. Hawley, chief train dispatcher; W. L. Wells, passenger agent; B. J. Cato, freight agent. Offices at depot. Tel. 162-B.

ᵢ**Western New York and Pennsylvania Railroad Company,** John McKarnes, passenger and freight agent. Office at depot. Tel. 87.

Bradford, Bordell and Kinzua Railway Company, John C. Mc-
Kenna, general manager, freight and passenger agent;
A. B Campbell, acting auditor and treasurer. Offices,
foot Chestnut. Tel. 208.

Allegheny and Kinzua Railway Company, M. D. Murray, superintendent; J. B. Murray, freight agent. Office at depot. Tel. 174.

Sugar Run Railroad Company, C. V. Merrick, superintendent;
M. D. Murray, assistant superintendent. Office at A.
& K. railroad depot. Tel 174.

Bradford and Western Pennsylvania Railway Company, C. S.
Whitney, president: W. F. Davis, vice president; W.
W. Bell, treasurer: P. H. Whitney, secretary and
general freight agent; N. A. Cole, superintendent.
General office, 5 St. James Place. Tel. 128.

Valley Railway Company, C. A. Weed. president; E. R.
Schoonmaker, vice president: J. H. Beardsley, general
manager; S A. Mundy, auditor and general freight
agent. General offices, Pompelon Hall. Tel. 160.

Ketner, St. Mary's and Shawmut Railway Company, S. A. Mundy,
president; S. T. Swartz. secretary; C. A. Weed,
treasurer; J. H. Beardsley, general manager: E. M.
Bell, auditor and general freight agent. General
offices, Pompelon Hall. Tel. 160.

Mt. Jewett and Cleremont Railway Company, B. F. Hazelton,
president; E. F. Clark, vice president; F. P. Hazelton, secretary and auditor; Edwin E. Tait, treasurer
and general manager; A. G. McComb' chief engineer.
General offices, 5 Producers' Exchange.

Mt. Jewett & Smethport Railroad Company, B. F. Hazelton,
president; Edwin F. Clark, vice president: F. P.
Hazelton, secretary and auditor; Edwin E. Tait,
treasurer and general council; A. G. McComb, chief
engineer. General offices, 5 Producers Exchange.

Kishwaukee Mineral Spring Railroad Company, James Pierce,
president; J R. Droney, general manager; W. R. Page,
secretary and treasurer; W. P. Pierce, auditor: C. W.
Wallis, general freight agent; M. G. Fitzpatrick,
superintendent. Bradford office 20 Davis block. 21
Main.

Olean, Rock City and Bradford Railway Company, Isaac B.
White, superintendent. Office 1 Main. Cor. Mechanic.
Tel. 270.

Bradford Electric Street Railway Company, Isaac B. White,
superintendent. Office 1 Main, cor. Mechanic. Tel.
270.

REAL ESTATE.

A. Balton, Over 38 Main.

L. W. Oakes, Agent Newell estate. Room A, Newell building. 98-100 Main.

A. W. Newell, 21 Congress.

A. J. Edgett, 1 Congress. Tel. 125.

C. B. Whitehead, 155 Jackson ave.

L. V. Devinney, Over 7 Main.

94

P. M. Berwald, Broker in oil properties, 1 Congress. Tel. 125.

P. L. & F. M. Webster, 37 Corydon. Tel. 130-B.

United Real Estate Company, W. J. Vallely, manager, 115½ Main.

L. L. Clough, 14 Moore block, 88 Main.

New Orange Industrial Association, C. M. Tompkins, president; M. H Arnott, treasurer; H. H. Hallock, secretary; C. W. Manahan, general manager; F. J. Ward, manager Western Pennsylvania. Office, 83 Main.

Charles J. Tremaine, Real estate. Money loaned. 17 Mechanic.

Loyal Ward, Real estate and collections. Over 81 Mechanic.

RESTAURANTS.

Option House, 39 Main. Tel. 263.

Vienna Cafe, 83 Main. Tel. 152.

The Rochester, 155 Main. Tel. 187.

The Capitol Restaurant and Cafe, James Murty, proprietor. Open all night. 40-42 Main.

Half-Dime Restaurant, N. W. McCourt, propr. Open all night. 76 Main.

Oil City House, 106-108 Main. Tel. 180.

Union House, 126 Main.

The Crystal Restaurant, W. A. Sykes, propr. Open night and day. Quick lunch for all trains. Ladies' dining parlor attached. 154 Main, near B. R. & P. depot.

Geo. B. Abbey, Lunch room. 389 East Main.

Joseph Newcomb, Restaurant and billiard room. 418 East Main.

O'Donnell & Eygabroat (James O'Donnell, A. W. Eygabroat), First-class restaurant and cafe. Restaurant open all night. 68 Mechanic, cor. Washington.

The Oyster Bay, A. H. Reed, propr. Oysters and clams a specialty. 115 Washington. Tel. 149-B.

Nelson's Restaurant, N. P. Nelson, propr. Ladies' and gent's dining room. 83-85 Mechanic.

The Williamson Cate, J. B. Jayne, propr. Ladies' and gent's dining room. Meals at all hours. 6-8 Congress. Tel. 221.

Model Restaurant, A. H. Wilcox, propr. Ladies' and gent's dining room. Open all night. 137 Main.

O'Neill's Restaurant, Con. O'Neill, propr. 116 Washington.

Klondike Restaurant, F. J. Freeman, propr. 10 St. James place.

SECOND-HAND DEALERS.

J. M. Burchfield, Furniture, stoves, etc., 21-23 Chestnut.

W. A. Hutchinson, Second-hand goods of all descriptions, 97 Main.

SEWING MACHINES.

L. Emery, Jr., & Co., 43-45 Main. (See hardware.)

White Sewing Machines, Gus Swanson, agent, 4 Congress.

Singer Manufacturing Company, L. E. Reed, agent Singer Sewing Machines and machine supplies of all kinds. 7 Congress.

Domestic Sewing Machines, Jos. W. Fritts, agent, over 5 Kennedy.

SLATE DEALERS.

New York Slate Quarries, Builders' slate. John J. Lane, agent. 30 Boylston.

STENOGRAPHERS.

Miss Margaret Vorce, Stenographer and typewriter, 1 Congress. Tel. 125.

Mrs. Bertha W. Howe, Stenographer and notary public. Washburn House, 84 Corydon. Tel. 14.

STONE YARD.

Kelly Bros. (David J., Thomas F.), Stone contractors and dealers. Yards, Elm and Erie railroad.

TABLE RELISHES,

E. L. Appleby & Co., P. E. Appleby, manager. Manufacturers and bottlers of home-made ketchup and all table relishes. 65 Congress.

TEA COMPANIES.

The Great American and Pacific Tea Company, C. G. Crouse, manager. Teas, coffees, spices, flavoring extracts, china and glassware. 101 Mechanic.

The Union Pacific Tea Company, J. W. Johnson, manager. Teas, coffees. spices and baking powder. China and glassware. 105 Main.

TEACHERS OF DANCING.

Slone's Dancing School, Mr. and Mrs. R. H. Slone, teachers of all kinds of dances. Class meets every Wednesday evening from 8 to 10 at Exchange Lyceum. Reception first Wednesday evening of every month from 10 to 12:30. in Lyceum.

Prof. H. F. Smith, Teaches all the latest dances. Dancing class meets every Monday evening at Pompelon Hall. Reception every fourth Monday in month. Office, rear 61 Main.

M. T. Gilligan, Teacher of stage and fancy dancing, 42 Corydon.

TEACHERS OF LANGUAGES AND ELOCUTION.

Ida W. Chapman, Teacher of elocution, 156 Corydon.

Mrs. H. Tschachtli, Teacher of French, 90 School.

BOVAIRD & SEYFANG

MANUFACTURING COMPANY,

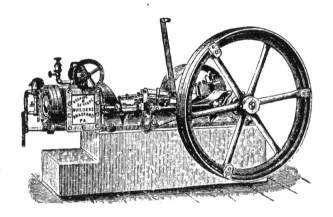

BRADFORD, PA., U. S. A.

MANUFACTURERS OF

Drilling and Fishing Tools

Boilers, Engines, Rig Irons, &c,

OIL, GAS *and* ARTESIAN WELL SUPPLIES.

MANUFACTURERS OF

THE "B. & S." GAS ENGINES.

BRANCH OFFICE AND WORKS:

PITTSBURGH, PA.

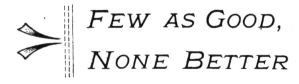

FEW AS GOOD,

NONE BETTER

......THAN THE......

Bradford Steam Laundry

11, 13, 15, 17 and 19 Bishop Street,

BRADFORD, PA.

—

FREEMAN & KATHAN, PRORIETORS.

—

Unequalled Facilities

For All Kinds of Laundry Work,

—

Family Washing by the Pound or Piece.

—

Carpet Cleaning and
Lace Curtain Work

A SPECIALTY.

—

A TRIAL ORDER SOLICITED.

TEACHERS OF VOCAL AND INSTRUMENTAL MUSIC.

Miss Kathryne A. Seyfang, Teacher of piano forte and theory. (Pupil of Arthur Foote.) Tuesdays, Wednesdays, Fridays and Saturdays at studio. Room 18, Exchange Lyceum, 35 Main.

Isabel M. Buton. Voice culture. (Pupil of Signor Rotoli and Signor Olivieri.) Mondays and Thursdays at studio, 18 Exchange Lyceum, 35 Main.

Prof. J. B. Hopley, Teacher of piano, organ and voice culture. Studio, Room 7, Berry & Melvin block, 18 Main.

E. E. Ellison, Teacher of violin and mandolin. Studio, 161 Jackson ave.

Prof. Alexander Johnston, Teacher of music. All string and brass instruments. 35 years' experience. Studio, over 16 Pine.

Mrs. Eva M. Bell, Teacher of piano and harmony. Studio, 27 Chautauqua Place.

Miss Nettie A. Hovey, Teacher of piano forte. Studio, 23 Jellerson.

Mrs. Nellie Hibler, Teacher of voice culture and piano forte. Studio, 18 Thompson ave.

Mrs. C. W. Lockard, Vocal instructor and contralto. Studio. 26 Elm

Miss Ray A. Mayer, Teacher of piano forte. Studio, 101 Centre. .

Miss Clementine Wise, Teacher of piano forte and pipe organ. Studio, 33 Foreman.

Miss Ella Long, Teacher of piano forte. 62 Pleasant.

Mary J. Donohue, Teacher of piano forte, 11 Foreman.

A. J. & Emma A. Durand, Teachers of piano, banjo, mandolin and guitar. 39 Kennedy

Miss Lottie E. Hall, Teacher of piano forte, 43 Amm.

Arthur C. Scheffer, Teacher of violin, 115 Centre.

Miss Ella Pifer, Teacher of piano, 295 East Main.

Frank J. Fuller, Teacher of Piano, 57 High.

Miss Ola P. Smathers, Teacher of piano, 151 High.

Mrs. Neilie Pixley, Teacher of piano forte and theory. Saturday afternoons at studio, 78 Elm.

Miss Georgia Hall, Teacher of piano forte. Studio, 99 Mechanic

Mrs. Nellie S. Pettit, Vocal and instrumental. Studio, 21 Mechanic.

Miss Adelaide Cohen, Teacher of piano. Studio, over 91 Main.

Jake Sorrentino, Teacher of guitar and mandolin, 110 Main.

E. Sorrentino, Teacher of guitar, 12 Congress.

Miss Florence E. Mayer, Teacher of piano forte. Studio, 101 Centre.

TELEGRAPH AND TELEPHONE COMPANIES.

Western Union Telegraph Company, E. E. Buel, manager. Office in Exchange Lyceum. Right hand side of hall. 35 Main. Tel. 210.

Postal Telegraph and Cable Company, F. M. Kelleher, manager. Office in Exchange Lyceum. Left hand side of hall. 35 Main. Tel. 201.

New York & Pennsylvania Telephone and Telegraph Company, George L. Lawrence, manager. Third floor, 53 Main. "Hello Central."

TICKET BROKERS.

Gibson & Mulcay (C. R. Gibson, J. W. Mulcay), Earle .. Tarbox, agent. Tickets and mileage bought and sold to all parts of the country. Also steamship tickets to all foreign countries. Office 121 Main, Riddell house block.

W. G. Palmer & Co., Agents for White Star and Anchor line ocean steamers. Tickets to all parts of Great Britain, Continental Europe, Africa, New South Wales and Australia. Office 130 Main. Tel. 177.

Robert Bauer, Agent for the American. North German Lloyd, Cunard, Anchor, Allen and Red Star Line, and Cook's Tourists' Agency. Also agent for Knauth Nachod Kuhne, foreign bankers, and C. B. Richard & Co. foreign bankers. Office 6 Public Square.

TIN, SHEET-IRON AND COPPERSMITHS.

Louis Tschachtli, Tin. sheet iron and copper woker, 47 Mechanic.

J. M. Stevenson, Manufacturer and dealer in tin and copper ware, 10 Congress.

Geo. A. Bodine, Tin, copper and sheet iron work, 98-100 Mechanic. Tel. 232.

J. B. Fox, Tin, sheet iron and copper work. Builders' tin a specialty. 60 Main and 2-4 Chestnut. Tell. 111.

T. M. Griffith & Son, Tin and sheet metal workers. 165 Main. Tel. 122-B.

TORPEDOES, NITRO-GLYCERINE AND DYNAMITE.

Newton Torpedo Company (C. F. Newton, H. G. Barcroft, Delevan Emery), Torpedoes and nitro-glycerine. Office, 135 echanic. Tel. 185.

Bradford Torpedo Company (George H. Dana. J. L. Adams), Manufacturers of and dealers in torpedoes and pure nitro-glycerine. Office, room 1, over 36 Main. Tel. 104. Torpedo barn and tin shop, 86 Chestnut. Barn tel. 264.

Rock Glycerine Company, R. A. Dempsey, manager. Manufacturers of and dealers in powder, caps, fuse, nitro-glycerine, torpedoes and dynamite Works at Howard Junction. Office, over 46 Main, Rosenberg & Michael block. Tel. 112.

Atlantic Dynamite Company, of New Jersey, M. G. Raub, agent. Room 4, Masonic Temple, 73 Main. Tel. 267.

Hercules Powder Company, of Wilmington, Del. M. G. Raub, agent. Room 4, Masonic Temple, 73 Main. Tel. 267.

W. D. Burdick, Dealer in nitro-glycerine and torpedoes. Office, Riddell House. cor. Main and Davis. Tel. 262.

Repanne Chemical Company, of Wilmington, Del. High explosives. M. G. Raub, agent. Room 4, Masonic Temple, 73 Main. Tel. 267.

TRANSPORTATION AND STORAGE COMPANIES.

J. J. Cole, Fire-proof storage warehouse and barns, cor. Barbour and Water. Office. 99 Main. Tel. 247-B.

Bisett Bros. (E. W., W. W. and J. J.), Fire-proof warehouse and barns, rear 43 Congress. Office, 19 Webster. Tel. 214.

UNDERTAKERS.

C. J. Lane, Undertaker and embalmer. Also agent for Lovell Diamond Bicycles. 4 Boylston. Tel. 142.

Otto Koch, Funeral director and embalmer. 139-141 South Mechanic. Tel. 129.

D. H. Rook & Co., (David H. Rook, Victor Gray), Undertakers and embalmers. 32 Chestnut. Tel. 105.

UPHOLSTERERS.

F. E. Kathan, Furniture repairing. Carpet and awning work, etc , 136 South Mechanic.

William Francis, Upholstering and carpet laying, rear 16 Public Square.

R. B. Hale, Mattress making and upholstering, 50 Elm.

VARIETY STORES.

B. Rosenthal, 5c and 10c store, 27 Main.

W. D. Hatch, 5c and 10c stores, at 61 Main and 91 Mechanic.

J. B. Goodliff, 5c and 10c store, 70 Mechanic.

VETERINARY SURGEONS.

W. S. Clark, D. V. S., Office and hospital, 23 Barbour.

Dr. C. Smith, D. V. S., Office and hospital, 16 Barbour.

WALL PAPER AND HOUSE DECORATIONS.

Bradburn & Chisholm (Clinton L. Bradburn, Alonzo C. Chisholm), dealers in wall paper, window shades, draperies, house decorations of all kinds, and art materials. Paints and varnishes. 95 Main, Bradburn block.

Chappell's Art Store, E. B. Chappell, propr. Wall paper and picture frames. Also painting, graining and sign writing. 12 Boylston.

Zook & Co. (John R. and Joseph Zook), Wall paper, window shades. Oil cloths, feathers and paints 14 Chestnut.

Racket Store, Wall paper, window shades. oil cloths 6 to 14 Kennedy.

Geo. W. Huntington, Wall paper. Painting and paper hanging. 8 Chambers.

F. E. Bradley. Sole agent for Alfred Peats' prize wall paper. 38 Main.

MISCELLANEOUS.

Business Addresses which Were Received Too Late to Come Under Proper Heading.

Ed. G. Bachtell, Dealer in ladies' and gents' fine footwear. 102 Mechanic, next to Mansion House.

Haines & Stewart (E. F. Haines, J. T. Stewart. successors to Charles F. Newton), Livery, boarding and feed stables. 135-137 Mechanic. Tel. 185

HAVE YOU SEEN IT?

......THE......

Petroleum Gazette.

The only independent journal circulating among oil men throughout the entire regions and among dealers generally.

Its mission is to keep the oil men informed on all matters pertaining to their interests, and at the same time make a decent living for its publishers.

ONE DOLLAR A YEAR AND WORTH IT.

Send for sample copies or a year's subscription to

GAZETTE PUBLISHING CO., Titusville, Pa.

CONTENTS OF THE BOOK.

CPSIA information can be obtained
at www.ICGtesting.com
Printed in the USA
BVHW05s2120090418
512843BV00030B/1696/P